T0195565

Other titles by Don Levin you may enjoy

The Code

Knight's Code

Broken Code

The Gazebo
The Life Story of Alexander Lebenstein

Eight Points of the Compass

Don't Feed the Bears

Another Last Day

The Advocate
(sequel to Another Last Day)

Blast of Trumpets

Also

Wisdom of the Diamond
(with Tom Bartosic)

The Leader Coach
(with Terry Edwards)

The Right Combination
(with Todd Bothwell)

Visit our website at donlevin.com

Clarion Blast

Quotes for a Lifetime

Don Levin

authorHOUSE®

AuthorHouse™
1663 Liberty Drive
Bloomington, IN 47403
www.authorhouse.com
Phone: 1 (800) 839-8640

Published by AuthorHouse 04/08/2019

ISBN: 978-1-7283-0671-1 (sc)
ISBN: 978-1-7283-0670-4 (e)

Library of Congress Control Number: 2019903974

Print information available on the last page.

To my heroine and muse…. Susie.
For being an example of:
enduring to the end,
unconditional love to all our children and grandchildren,
unquestioning faith,
and living a covenant life.
Thanks for being along for the Journey and
keeping me on the correct path.

CONTENTS

PREFACE

Over the years, as I have both read and written a great deal, I compiled quite a collection of quotes from a wide range of people. These quotes and this collection of people ranged from great scholars and leaders, to simple ordinary people whom I knew personally. These quotes served as a *Blast of Trumpets* to me and as such I assembled them into a manuscript that while seemingly self-indulgent, also was intended to serve as a reference point from which the bedrock of my attitude and character was formed. It was also intended to hopefully serve as part of my legacy. After completing *Another Last Day* and its sequel *The Advocate,* two very personal stories reduced to fiction, I also realized that I wanted to share more of myself with my growing progeny.

I was very excited about the concept of the collection contained within *Blast of Trumpets*, and with great anticipation, shared it with my regular publisher who also was excited with the project. Imagine my surprise when after submitting the completed manuscript, the review team indicated that they wanted me to dilute the content of that collection by adding a lot of my own original thoughts! While there were no issues with copyright laws or attribution, an internal company rule about originality content reared its ugly head. In other words, even though the vast majority of the quotes contained within these pages are part of the public domain and free of copyright issues in their utilization, the publisher wanted more "original" content from me before they would set it to print. It was my choice as to whether to delete material and/or add that much more of my own.

For this reason, and this reason alone, I was forced to go back to journals, e-mails, and other correspondence in which I may have shared what I hoped would serve as a bit of inspiration. I started to merge these words into the original manuscript and was very unhappy with the result. I didn't want *Blast of Trumpets* to be about me. So, after getting fairly deep into another draft, I realized that I had done nothing but dilute the very purpose of the original work, so it was back to square one, and off to an alternative publisher with that project in its original format.

As a result, and looking to make lemonade out of lemons, I reviewed this new collection of "original" quotes and writings, and a thought began to germinate, and some excitement built within me. The only question was could I really publish a book of my own thoughts and observations without having my kids think that I had become a total narcissist or at a minimum pretty full of myself?

When a few of them either shrugged or said that it might be "kinda cool for the grandkids" I felt like I had been granted the necessary license to proceed with the project. When a few of my professional associates and friends also encouraged the project, I became even more comfortable with the concept. So, with a different perspective and renewed energy, it was once again back to the personal journals, archived e-mails, church talks, and scraps of paper under paperweights on my desk and even a notebook or two of original writings, and this is the result…an independent collection of my own thoughts. I hope you like it and that some part of it even resonates with you as it has with me as I assembled it.

DJL

"Make your own Bible. Select and collect all the words and sentences that in all your readings have been to you like the blast of a trumpet."

Ralph Waldo Emerson

"The nightingale has a lyre of gold,
The lark's is a clarion call,
And the blackbird plays but a boxwood flute,
But I love him best of all."

William Ernest Henley

Seasons

Code of Summer
If we are born in the Spring of Life,
And retire and enjoy the golden colors of the Fall,
To die in the deepening snows of Winter,
Then the season in which we are adults and rear
our children is the Summer of our lives.
The Code of Summer is the set of natural laws that govern our ability
to endure the trials and tribulations that we face from the Adversary
as we strive to raise our children in a spirit of righteousness and
to make Tomorrow better than was Today for those around us.
DJL
June 1995

"Spring is the season of re-birth and unlimited potential.
It must be why as an optimist that I love it so..."

"They say that 40 is the new 30. That 70 is the new 65. As I approach 60, I realize that the triple digits of summer heat are fading. The early morning dawn that often peaked its head above the horizon long before the newspaper would smack the front porch is now coming later, prompting the two dogs to sleep later as well. The sun that filled the western skies until nearly the late news broadcast has receded and it is now darker earlier in the evening. Clearly the change in seasons is beginning anew. Friends of our age as well as icons of our generation are being either slowed or felled by illness and infirmity like mighty oaks falling in the forest. Soon the leaves on the deciduous trees will turn color and begin their descent to the lawn below, marking the passing of another set of seasons. Summer is slowly but surely surrendering to Fall. We must begin to pray that the Fall will be kind to us and that when the time comes, that the Winter which will inevitably follow, will be a mild one for us both before the final snows."

DJL

August 2018

"We are all expendable. None of us more important than another. Even the Lord's Prophet is not more important than you or I. When he too is used up, with life's essence squeezed out of him like the last remnants of a tube of toothpaste, he too is called home. For when all is said and done, we really are all equal in that we are mortal and mere children of Heavenly parents. The question therefore is not how long we live, but how long our legacy will survive when our spirit has left our earthly body much like a hand leaves a glove. Our children and now grandchildren ARE our legacy. Yes, the books written are a lasting legacy as well, but the certificates on the wall, the awards and decorations, and all the other accolades of men really are quite meaningless when all is said and done. It really comes down to our character and that which we instill in our family that determines our usefulness in the Circle of Life."

"There is still so much smoke in the air as the jet stream carries it to Idaho from Oregon, Washington, and even from as far away as California. The orange sun is an eerie omen of the flames that are consuming tens of thousands of acres of forest. Forests dying, leaving blackened husks as testaments to the fury of nature. As time passes, there is surety in the knowledge that Mother Nature will see to their rebirth. Thousands of little seedlings spread their arms skyward towards the warmth of the sun as they will soon stand shoulder to shoulder on the same ground as the passage of time occurs."

"Now is the season for me to engage in family history work. Since I have often heard that three generations are the approximate length of time before family lore is consumed and lost forever if it is not recorded, I know that it is my charge to be the linchpin or connecting link between generations future and past."

"I am at the finish line, the race at an end. There is neither fanfare nor ceremonial gold watch, but at the finish line I am. The absence of the next brass ring is liberating, as there now only remain new vistas to be explored and conquered in the name of passion, growth, and legacy."

"Can there be anything more delightful than a cool crisp morning where the warmth of the sun battles with the cool breeze of the wind that blows through my hair as I drive my car with the top down en route to an act of service."

ABUNDANCE

"If all you care about in the course of your life is money, you will be sadly unrewarded."

"Fame and fortune will never bring you abundance, for like happiness, it is really an intangible that originates from within ourselves."

"I've known people who were not rich financially but happy in the rest of their lives."

"I am not sure that it takes money to be truly happy if we are counting the right things."

"While all happy people are not necessarily generous, I have never met a generous person who is also not happy. I guess happiness really is all a state of mind."

"There will always be people who have more than you, just as there will be those who marvel at the riches you possess. The key to a life of abundance is to be grateful for your own lot in life, and to live your life in that manner."

"Buy nice cars when they are two years old, having suffered the worst of the depreciation, and then reap the benefits."

"People who express gratitude on a regular basis are not only happier and healthier, but also live lives filled with abundance."

"Abundance is a state of mind that we achieve through the practice of gratitude."

"Abundance is all about believing that you have everything that you really need and want. Everything else becomes icing on the cake."

"Abundance is not about 'stuff' or possessions. It is about achieving a tranquility in our soul."

Achievement

"The negativity of cynics limits their achievement while the questions of the skeptical are like anchors that keep them rigidly moored at the pier, never to enjoy the rewards and adventures of the blue ocean."

"The manner in which we approach a task will often dictate whether we achieve the success we desire."

"Apply the Power of One in your life and do more than is required of you to do in every situation. The progress you achieve will exceed all of your expectations."

"It is attention to detail and the little things that allow us to progress from good to great."

"Big achievements start with small ones."

"There are four steps to achievement:
Plan Purposefully.
Prepare prayerfully.
Proceed Positively.
Pursue persistently."

"Not trying is worse than any failure."

"Achievement starts with the first step of the journey."

"Don't waste a minute of time. Make sure that you are investing your time on something worthwhile and not simply spending time in idle pursuits."

"Live in such a way that the little things do not escape your attention."

"Achievement begins by taking small steps that transform dreams into actions."

"Sometimes I think achievement is simply a euphemism for persistence or tenacity."

Action

"We create our legacy each day with even small acts."

"The end of one race does not have to be the start of the next one."

"If fear is a lack of preparation, then be prepared, and fear not!"

"Life is about taking action because our actions dictate our ultimate destination."

"People may not always believe what you say, but they will always believe what you do. It is all about walking the walk and not just talking the talk."

"Don't confuse busy work with action."

"Just jump in the pool. It doesn't matter what stroke you are doing, so long as you are swimming. Action is the differentiator between dreams and goals."

"You can read every book, see every movie, on whatever subject... let's say baseball. But until you get on the field and you are throwing the ball, catching the ball, swinging the bat, and running the bases, it is nothing more than theory. You have to cross the chalk lines and get on the field and participate in the game."

"Don't wish for it. Work for it!"

"I learned a long time ago that we are given a finite amount of time on this Earth. For some it can span a century or more; for others it may be only a blink of an eye. I also learned that one cannot 'manage' time, and that it is really all about how we utilize the time that is allotted to us. Some claim that multi-tasking is the way to maximize time; I used to do that on a regular basis, e.g. watch television, read a book, and talk to my wife, more or less simultaneously. I have since realized that there really is no such thing as multi-tasking. We can *alternate* from tasks seemingly being performed simultaneously, but truth be told, we really can do only one thing at a time. As a result, it is about prioritizing our actions. The following is one of my favorite stories about this thing that people like to refer to as time management.

One day an expert in time management was speaking to a group. He pulled out a one gallon, wide mouthed jar and set it on the table in front of him. He also produced about a dozen fist-sized rocks and carefully placed them, one at a time, into the jar. When the jar was filled to the top and no more rocks would fit inside, he asked, "Is this jar full?" Everyone in the group quickly responded with "yes." He then reached under the table and pulled out a bucket of gravel. He then dumped some gravel in and shook the jar, causing pieces of gravel to settle down

into the spaces between the rocks. He then again
asked the group, "Is the jar full?"
But this time some of the group was hesitant to
respond, unsure of the proper answer.
"Good," he said as he reached under the table and this time
brought out a bucket of sand and dumped a good portion of it
into the jar. Once more he asked the question, "Is the jar full?"
This time, no one answered.
He then grabbed a pitcher of water and poured it in until
the jar was finally filled to the brim. He looked at the
class and asked, "What's the point of this exercise?"
One person viewing the exercise said, "The point is,
no matter how full your schedule is, if you really think
about it, you can always fit more things in it."
"No," replied the speaker with a smile. "That's not the point. That's
what most people think. The truth this exercise teaches is that if you
don't put the big rocks in first, you'll never get them in at all."

So, what are the big rocks in your life – the PRIORITIES?
It should be your family, your faith, as well as worthy
cause or two, and a hobby that helps you grow.
Remember to put these in first or you'll never get them in at all."

"A vision is like a movie. It is something that you feel and is constantly changing. It is a living, breathing ideal that dictates your actions."

"I love to whiteboard things and let my mind run wild because I know that these ideas will turn into actions which will in turn become success."

Attitude

"If you think you can't do something, you are probably right. If you attempt the seemingly impossible, you may just surprise yourself with the results."

"You can't control someone else's attitude, merely your own."

"Life is all about how we react to those things that we do not control."

"Your countenance is a looking glass into your soul."

"We are only a positive mental attitude away from the success that we all crave."

"The past and the future are both beyond our reach; for this reason, we must place our best efforts into the present."

"Half empty, half full. You will be right half the time, depending on your attitude."

"We can change the outcome of our lives by changing our attitude."

"I am but one. I cannot change the world, but I can certainly control how I allow the world to impact me."

"Tomorrow is always full of promise and new opportunities...if we but open our eyes."

"Confidence allows us to accomplish anything we set our minds to doing."

"Our outside as viewed by the world is typically merely a mirror image of our insides as we craft them."

"We have the power to change ourselves
one belief, one action, at a time."

"Is there any greater waste of talent than a young
child with a pessimistic attitude?"

Our perceptions often defy reality – we are a byproduct
of our past and of our environment – for this reason,
our eyes do not always see what is really there."

"I have had many people take me to task for my optimism. I figure if that is the worst thing that they can call me on, I am okay with that; nobody wants to be with, much less follow, a negative leader."

"Our destiny is often dictated by the seemingly insignificant day-to-day decisions we make as much as the seemingly momentous ones over which we can sometimes agonize."

"We are always going to be tested; the key is in how we respond."

"We are not as imperfect or inferior as others would attempt to make us believe. Conversely, those we encounter are decidedly not as perfect as they may themselves believe or attempt to make us believe."

"We can't change other people, much less the past. We can't change the inevitable. What we can change is our attitude, and how we react to these other things."

"A bad attitude is like bad breath. Nobody wants to share it with you."

"Left unattended, a poor attitude can become
a deficit in your character."

"Your attitude can in fact become one of your
greatest tools towards achieving success."

"A dying person's will to live is probably the most
powerful positive attitude that I have ever observed."

"Attitude contributes fare more to our individual and team successes than does either skills or knowledge."
Wisdom of the Diamond

"It is about executing on fundamentals all the while doing so with the proper attitude that will serve as a force multiplier."

"Attitude dictates most of our success."

Change

"Life is like Underwear…Change is good."

"We should always be committed to self-improvement…right up until the day we die."

"Only you can change your life. Don't wait for someone else to do it."

"Grandma Mary always emphasized the importance of attaining a college education; impressing upon us that it was the most impactful way to change our lives for the better."

"Change is a constant over which we can exercise control if we embrace it."

"Remember that progress is impossible without change; which is why we should be agents of change and fully embrace it."

"A kind word or act of encouragement can often be enough to spark change within the hearts of others."

"Ignorance always opposes change. Don't be ignorant."

"If we resist change, we resist the opportunity to grow. Failure to grow leaves us no alternative other than stagnation and eventually death."

"Change is scary for most people. Fear of the unknown can cause people to remain completely sedentary. How liberating it is when we embrace change and see it as an agent of progress."

"In terms of change, it is all about embracing it mentally before you attempt it physically."

"I know people who absolutely abhor change. Years ago, it was easy to avoid; life was not anywhere near as fast-paced as it is today. If you are part of the world today, you must realize that change will be a constant companion."

Character

"Our character is the outward reflection of our inner attitudes."

"Our character truly defines the person we are and ever hope to be in this life."

"Our character is a history of our past, a billboard of our present, and the seer of all our potential futures. We must insure that we do nothing to harm it."

"Our character can be a magnet that attracts people, or the greatest repellant."

"Character takes a lifetime to build, and only a moment to lose."

"Our character is best reflected when we are in engaged in activities that we might not otherwise want to cast for ourselves."

"Resiliency is all about how we react to one of Life's inequities."

"Life was not intended to be fair. Our character can be best judged by how we react to the inequities that we encounter in our sojourn through life."

"The true hero is the person who rises above the tumult and perseveres to achieve even in the face of continued adversity."

"There is a lot being written about global warming and the effects that pollution and man's cruelty to the environment is having on our planet. Much the same can be said about the environment, or character, that we create in our own hearts. Our beliefs, actions, and character are the factors that determine the nature of our own personal climate."

"We cannot afford to compartmentalize our lives. We must be consistent in our words, deeds, and thoughts."

"While we can 'fake it until we make it' this does not apply to our character. Either we have it or we don't."

"We are responsible for setting the standards by which we will live our lives. There may be rules and regulations to follow, but whether they are reflected in our character and behavior is completely up to us."

"Is my outer countenance reflective of my true inner self?"

"Are my actions in congruence with, and reflective of, my character?"

"Many times, as child I was left to my own devices and lost myself in a book. Who would have imagined that in the process that I would also find myself?"

"Our character is the only thing we take with us from this life."

"You can't fake character. It is as real as the nose on your face, and just as visible for everyone to see."

"While often elusive, when finally possessed, Patience strengthens the spirit, sweetens the temper, stifles anger, subdues pride, opens the heart, and bridles the tongue."

"In science for every action there is a reaction. In life, for every action there is a consequence. Our everyday challenge is to live our lives, conduct ourselves, and govern our actions so that all of the consequences of our actions are positive and bright."

"Our thoughts are formulated in our attitudes and our beliefs.
When our thoughts are infused with energy,
spirit and vision, they become actions.
Actions coupled with persistence and congruence become habits.
Habits honed long enough can become our character.
Character is what defines who we are and the legacy we leave."

"There is no such thing as a self-made man or woman. We are all the byproduct of those who have influenced us from the time we are young and impressionable until the day we draw our last breath. If we are honest with ourselves, we must acknowledge all those people who have either inspired us, planted a seed, opened the door of opportunity, shared a kind word, validated us or an idea, provided encouragement, helped us find our true North or even simply pointed us in the right direction with a pat on the back."

"Your words reveal a great deal about yourself. Your willingness to serve others does as well. Linking your words with action defines your character."

"Our character is shaped not only by those with whom we interact but also by those who have preceded us, even if by hundreds of years. For those of us who love history and find solace, comfort, and even pride in quoting leaders of the past, literary giants like Emerson and Shakespeare, courageous leaders like Lincoln and Roosevelt, and inspiring figures such as Mandela and Gandhi, we must pay these people their just due. They have shaped and influenced us as much as any teacher or mentor with whom we have crossed paths."

"Many years ago, I read somewhere (and I have not been able to find the source) that the ancient Greeks said that 'character is destiny.' When I first read it and wrote it down on one of my countless scraps of paper, I didn't fully grasp the concept. With the passage of time I have a somewhat better understanding of it, and now believe it to mean that just as there are no coincidences, and things just don't simply happen. Case in point, the founding fathers of this country were not born when they were simply by chance; it was their *destiny* to exercise their *character* and to formulate the concepts associated with the Declaration of Independence and the birthright of this great country even at the very peril of their lives."

"Tattoos may be considered art, but Scars tell a story."

Courage

"I've always been reassured that Dante would be proven correct and that 'the hottest places in hell are reserved for those who, in the time of moral crisis, maintain their neutrality.' There is nothing worse in my mind that to stand there and do nothing when the very moral fabric of our society is being stretched to a breaking point. We must have the courage to stand up for what we believe to be Truth and right."

"Never say or do anything that compromises your integrity and reputation. What can be built in a lifetime can be lost in minutes."

"Courage is all about persevering especially in
the face of great loss and tragedy."

"Courage is largely habit and self-confidence.
First, decide what you want to be,
And then do what it takes to achieve it."
DJL September 2004

"Courage is not the absence of fear but the conquest of it."

"Amidst all the conferences I have attended over the years, I had the opportunity to attend the General Agent and Managers Association's (GAMA) meeting back in 2004, and one of our motivational speakers was a young man whom some of you may have seen on *Good Morning America* or other shows. His name is Kyle Maynard. What makes this 19-year-old University of Georgia freshman special? While a good student, and champion high school wrestler, he also just happens to have been born, because of a birth defect, with arms that end at the elbow, and legs that end at his knees. To say that we were stunned at the video clips of his wrestling *and football playing* prowess would be a huge understatement. This remarkable young man lost all the wrestling matches that he participated in for the first 18 months that he wrestled. Did this discourage him? No. His message to us was a very simple one: 'improve yourself each day … somehow.' He did and ended up with a record of 36-18 during his senior year as a varsity wrestler. While others may have adopted a life of handicapped privilege and self-pity, Kyle strives for normalcy in everything that he does, to include typing 50 words per minute on a standard keyboard. His example is nothing short of amazing. His final words of inspiration to us served as a reminder that we should 'never let our competitors determine how successful we will be – and that we need to grow from adversity.' While all of us have had adversity of some manner, shape, or form in our lives, I am relatively confident that we have not faced, nor had to overcome each and every day, anything like what this young man has done in his short life. So, whether it is picking up and dialing the phone, or processing leads, or a fear of asking for referrals, or tapping into your existing book of clients, or expanding your sphere of influence, look beyond the horizon, and become a possibility dreamer. This young man is a real example to us on how we should live our lives. As Mark Twain said, 'twenty years from now you will be more disappointed by the things you didn't do than by the ones you did. So, throw off the bowlines, sail away from the safe harbor. Catch the trade winds in your sails. Explore. Dream.' Make a promise to yourself that you too will be a champion."

"Dorothy wanted to go home… the Scarecrow wanted a brain… the Tinman wanted a heart in order to feel love, and the Lion wanted courage. In some ways, we are like all four of them; we all want to feel the security of home; the ability to think freely and be creative, and more importantly, to acquire knowledge – for knowledge is the only thing that we can take with us from this estate. We all want to be loved and to feel love, and finally, as men, we all want to think of ourselves as courageous warriors."

"I would like to return to the theme of courage again for a moment. I want to distinguish between physical courage and moral courage. As some of you know, I am still in the Army Reserve. I recently had occasion to talk to a friend of mine who served in Vietnam and managed to survive twenty-one fire fights in seventeen days, or in other words, he was forced on twenty-one separate challenges over seventeen days to face an enemy intent on taking his life. He was literally in kill-or-be-killed situations that continued to haunt him some thirty years later. He confirmed for me what I have often read about courage. Physical courage, such as that experienced in combat is often thrust upon us as any external force can be but is often simply reduced to self-preservation. As he shared with me, 'you sometimes do the crazy things that win you medals for bravery solely in an effort to save your own hide.' We continued to discuss the difference between physical and moral courage and agreed that moral courage could often be the more difficult courage to manifest, as it mostly certainly must come from within oneself. It requires a willingness to stand by one's convictions even in the face of physical danger. It requires a willingness to raise one's voice to be heard and can often have far reaching results of both a positive and negative nature."

"Most of us will never face an armed enemy or be faced with life threatening situations that will test our courage. Nonetheless, it takes courage to be obedient, and to do things we might not want to do ourselves, or things that might be construed as unpopular with friends, followers, and those around us. It is in these situations that we can manifest our own courage."

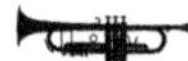

"I exhort you to look at your own family and I dare say that you will find that each one of you have something to be proud of in the way of a courageous ancestor. My ancestors had the courage to leave faraway lands for the promise of America. With no money, not speaking the language, they came. Until the day she died, my grandmother always held a special place for 'Lady Liberty' and Ellis Island in her heart. I am named for a hero of World War Two. He was a man who did not want to go to war but go he did. And despite initial prejudice against him from the very men with whom he was assigned to fight and labor, he earned the respect of those around him through countless acts of physical courage which ultimately cost him his life."

"Courage is doing what you find yourself afraid. If you are not afraid, there is no courage required."

"Isn't it amazing how courageous little league ballplayers are when they go to the plate. No fear, no angst, just the desire to swing the bat, and to earn a moment's glory."

"Courage is all about mastering those butterflies."

DREAMS

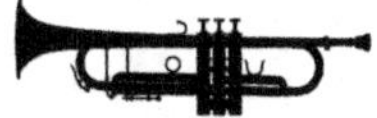

"Nobody has ever accused me of having small dreams."

"We can make virtually any dream come true if we have the perseverance to pursue them even in the face of adversity."

"Daydreaming is the precursor to actually DOING it."

"Is there anything grander than when a daydream becomes a reality?"

"If you can imagine it, stick with it, and overcome the challenges, your dreams can become your future."

"A successful man first dreams it."

"Dreaming can be an escape mechanism but also the bedrock from which success springs."

"Dreams are just your subconscious coming up for air and leaving you with additional thoughts to ponder."

"Dreams begin at home."

"Dreams can be indulgent…and pure fantasy when we indulge ourselves in a bit of Walter Mitty-esque self-aggrandizement… or can be our subconscious at work as our mind engages in possibility thinking and lays the foundation for future endeavors and success. They can also be a view of things yet to come, grounded in reality brimming with anticipation, when reality IS better than dreams."

"Dreaming is often the best part of life."

Excellence

"We are all imbued with God-given talents. Our challenge in life is to rise to the high-water mark of our true potential and to resist satisfying for something less."

"There is no governor on the gas pedal of life when we are in pursuit of excellence. Always do your best."

"There is no greater joy than that of exceeding
our own [modest] expectations."

"Make Perfection the goal but accept Excellence as the result."

"Remember, there is no speed limit in the pursuit of excellence!"

"A Champion does his best, and then a little more. In large part, each of us is a world-class athlete that challenges the physical, mental, and emotional paradigms thrust upon us by the world, each day in a very competitive environment. The Olympic ideal is about getting the very best from deep within our own inner being. Nobody ever conceived of a 4-minute mile, and yet after Roger Bannister *did* it, countless others have followed. The human condition allows us to apply our attitude and belief to our seemingly finite physical abilities and to do things swifter, higher, and stronger. Every one of us is an Olympic athlete running the marathon. That being said, we need to draw on our inner strength and convictions to get us over the rough spots, and to help us run through the wall of pain that we may encounter. Here are some tips on how to do it.

<u>Desire:</u> just do a little more; drive through the pain, stretch your capacity – live the Power of One.

<u>Individual Effort:</u> make yourself stronger based on your weaknesses, e.g. take your weaknesses, and turn them into strengths by working out hard.

<u>Faith in Yourself:</u> win before you run the event. Have self-confidence, and visualize yourself at the finish line, wearing the winner's wreath. Picture yourself standing in the winner's circle. It all starts with you!

<u>Be Honest with Yourself:</u> look people in their eyes – don't make excuses for yourself. Be responsible for yourself and your actions. No one is responsible for your success more than you!

<u>Discipline:</u> Cut out of your life those things that keep you from doing your best. Lose the negative energy drains. Don't flock with the turkeys, soar with the eagles. Stay in congruence.

<u>Expect Some Failures:</u> Always shoot for the stars, and settle for dragging your feet in the treetops, rather than aiming too low. Sometimes we must fall. Sadly, we most often learn more from our failures than our successes.

<u>Bounce Back to Victory:</u> Rise above the challenge. The bottom can be something that we merely bounce up from on our way to the top!
<u>Teamwork & Unity:</u> You can't applaud with one hand. Life is a cooperative venture."

"Excellence is not an attribute but rather an attitude. It has to come deep from within your own soul."

"I have always found that striving for excellence has been a great motivation. In other words, it is a lot more fun to make dust than it is to eat it."

Faith & Miracles

"Faith is the first principle in revealed religion, and the foundation of all righteousness."

"Just as you cannot be 'a little pregnant' – either you are, or you are not, so too with faith. Faith, and miracles for that matter, requires us to be all in."

"We must always align ourselves with Truth and Light."

"The spirit will whisper to you…
Be sure to follow thru."

"Doubt are the seeds sown by the Adversary.
We need to cling to those things that we know to be Truth.
You don't jump overboard during stormy weather."

"While looking for heroes, children – and that is all of us for that matter – would be better served to avoid celebrities and those in the limelight, and to look closer to home. For the real heroes of this life will be those who endure to the end while striving to do that which is righteous and of God."

DJL June 1994

"When the doctors and the laws of Nature seemingly conspire to dictate a certain [undesired] outcome, and the powers of prayer, faith, and hope, triumph joyfully, that is a miracle."

DJL

April 2012

"Angels are not confined to the Heavens above.
They can often be found walking amidst us."

"At the time we are baptized and confirmed, we are given the precious gift of the Holy Ghost as a companion; to guide us, to protect us, and to help us negotiate the path of Life. Nonetheless, it is incumbent upon us to invite the Spirit into our lives each day with constant and fervent prayer."

"Pray with thanksgiving foremost in your heart."

"The family file cards on my desk stare back at me, seemingly pleading for their time in the spotlight. More than just names, they are kindred spirits speaking to me, linking current and future generations to the past. I am once again a sentinel."

"Don't miss out on the steady everyday opportunity for revelation by waiting for the loud and spectacular."

"A picture found in the course of my family history research makes them more than a name or a distant relation. That picture makes them part of my family."

"I have had my heart broken many times in the course of doing my family history research...as their trials, travails, and often tragedies, seemingly became my own as well."

"Death is the universal destiny of all of us. None are immune. Fortunately, I now have knowledge and insight that death is neither an end or a state of being but rather a transition. While we all hope to meet it late in an otherwise long and rewarding life, some, even children, will face transition at an earlier time. How good it is to know that this temporary separation is just that: temporary, and that we will be together as an eternal family."

"It is important to know where you are at all times. Because of technology, you can rely on GPS to determine your physical location, but for spiritual and moral purposes it is up to you to maintain your equilibrium and location by deciding ahead of time what you will and won't do, what you will and won't condone, and what you hold to be Truth."

"It is equally important to know where you are going. The best way to do this is to maintain one eye directly in front of you looking for obstacles, and one eye locked on a fixed point on the horizon so that you don't lose your way."

"In the course of my own personal mortal ministry, I have attempted to gather as much knowledge and wisdom as possible that I might continue forward on my own eternal progression. Reading the teachings of the latter day prophets as well as figuratively sitting at their feet during our semi-annual General Conference, I have garnered many truths. Some of these truths from President Thomas S. Monson include:

- ❖ 'When God speaks and a man obeys, that man will always be right'.
- ❖ 'When you are on the Lord's errand, you are entitled to the Lord's help.'
- ❖ 'Whom the Lord calls, the Lord qualifies.'
- ❖ 'The door of history turns on small hinges, and so do people's lives.'

How else can I explain my ability to serve as a bishop and to magnify all the other callings to which I have been called? It truly is all about living our lives in such a manner that we can listen with our hearts as well as our ears and to be receptive to the promptings of the Holy Ghost which can often come as quietly as a whisper."

"Reason will never replace revelation. We need to do things during the week to strengthen our testimonies We need to "feel and give" the love of Heavenly Father in order to identify our divine nature. We can feel different by having influence with kids & grandkids by sharing prayers, blessings, and by being an example! Most importantly, we are not mortals attempting to have spiritual experiences, but we are in fact spiritual beings having a temporary mortal experience."

"What spiritual foundation is your testimony built upon? A man (Joseph Smith or Brigham Young, for example) or the Rock (the Savior). Where is your testimony really grounded? Is it built upon a rock or merely upon sand? I encourage you to Write down your spiritual experiences (I am capturing some of them in my novels). My spiritual foundation is built, with child-like faith, on the premise that the Savior lives today and because of his sacrifices, and, predicated on our faithfulness and obedience, we may return with Honor to live in celestial glory with our eternal family in the presence of Heavenly Father. This testimony is fueled by the *knowledge* of where we came from, why we are here, and where we are going when our probationary learning period here on the earth is concluded. I honestly believe that I am a spiritual being have a mortal experience rather than just a mortal being *hoping* to occasionally have a spiritual one."

"Recognizing that church service sometimes involves a lot of standing in the hallway waiting for the next leadership meeting to start…"

"Recognizing the synergy of power created by being equally yoked. Yoke yourself to your eternal companion and to the Savior."

"We must ponder, pray, and apply those Truths that we hold near and dear."

"When we are baptized and confirmed, we are commanded to receive the Holy Ghost. Or is it really a matter of being blessed with the gift of the Holy Ghost? The GIFT. And it truly is a gift. I have felt it, appreciate it, and know of the tremendous significance that it plays in my life."

"I also believe that I was aware of the Spirit even before I joined the church even if I did not have a perfect knowledge of it. I guess that is why when I did receive it, it was almost like finally being introduced to a long-time friend and companion whose name I had never known."

"We are clearly imperfect beings living in an even more imperfect world striving to learn those things that will allow us to return to live with our perfect Father in Heaven."

"Whether you *know* it or not, the Savior *is* in every detail of our lives if you take the time to notice..."

"Elder David O. McKay said that 'Man has a dual nature: one related to the earthly or animal life; the other, akin to the divine. Whether a man remains satisfied within what we designate the animal world, satisfied with what the animal world will give him, yielding without effort to the whim of his appetites and passions and slipping farther and farther into the realm of indulgence, or whether, through self-mastery, he rises toward intellectual, moral, and spiritual enjoyments depends upon the kind of choice he makes every day, nay, every hour of his life.' He said that in General Conference in 1949. Long before the rise of the Internet, or Playboy magazine, or the readier availability of drugs on the street, or the ability to enjoy nearly instant gratification of whatever else we may be seeking. We have all felt the tugs of Satan as he tempts us. Whether it is the Word of Wisdom, with a stray Coke, or cup of coffee, or glass of wine, or cigar, or overindulging at the buffet. It can be a challenge to our integrity in our business dealings, or simply not returning the extra change that the cashier gives to us in error. Conversely, it can simply be doing what we know is right; we have the GIFT of the Holy Spirit to help us, guide us, and to direct us on the correct path. I know with total certainty that when I follow the promptings that the Spirit places in my heart and conscience, that I am happier, feel better about myself, and that the feeling of connection to my Heavenly Father is strengthened."

"Death is just another step in our eternal progression."

"I was a *Magnum PI* aficionado. I really liked that show. It had all my favorite things: the military, guns, pretty girls, fast cars, Hawaii, mystery, and something unique: Magnum's little voice. He used to talk about it. He used to describe it. He used to tell us, the viewer, when and how it was whispering to him. I used to think, 'yeah, me too.' Of course, now, I know it was the Spirit. I guess the Spirit was also part of my true conversion to the Church because I already had a testimony of it as being an independent force in my universe. It was more than just a conscience; more than just a guiding light; more than a knowledge of black and white based on right and wrong. It was an infallible pillar of light blazing a trail for me through the darkness. It seems like I always got in trouble when I ignored my own little voice."

"When dealing with the Spirit, we have to remember that the Spirit speaks with words that we *feel* rather than hear. Sometimes these words are merely a prompting to act, to say something, or to do something. Sometimes these acts may be contrary to what we think or may leave us in a stupor of thought. No matter, it is cause to act."

"I remember the day that we were sealed in the Temple as an eternal family. The look of complete knowledge evident in the eyes of my fifteen month old daughter was enough to complete my conversion. Since that day I have often wondered how much different all our lives would be if we were each afforded only a furtive glance at our pre-mortal lives before we came to Earth. What if we were able to remember just a sliver of what we knew in the pre-existence? What impact would it have on the lives we endeavor to lead in our mortal probation? Would it be enough to help us not make all the bad choices that we sometimes find ourselves making either in ignorance or because of temptation by the Adversary? Would it provide us with more of an eternal perspective? Would such an experience make us more courageous and self-confident and afford us the strength to always stand up for Truth? Would we remember the covenants that we made and the true purpose of our time in this world? Would we remember the purpose of our Journey? Would it be the ultimate, 'oh yeah? Now I get it!' Just something to ponder."

"I am convinced that adversity is designed to make us more grateful for the good that we enjoy in our lives; less complacent, quicker to action, more obedient, more mindful of the covenants that we make in the Temple, and more acutely aware of the differences between good and evil, health and sickness, light and darkness, pleasure and pain. It also teaches us great patience, long suffering, about the power of prayer, and the necessity to achieve balance in our lives."

"We know that before we were born that we were coming to Earth for bodies and experiences necessary for our progression, and that we would have joys and sorrows, comforts and hardships, successes and disappointments, and we knew that after a period of life that we would die. We accepted these eventualities with a glad heart, because we knew that it was the way of the Lord."

"I know that I have grown as a person because of the adversity present in my life. I know much more fully now that you can't have a good day with a bad attitude, and that you can't have a bad day with a good attitude."

"All of us have daily trials and tribulations. Never under estimate the power of a kind word, of a smile, or act of kindness. Never become so caught up in your temporal life, or complacent about your spiritual growth to remember that the Adversary is always there, waiting for you to become lax."

"Albert Einstein once said 'in difficulty, find opportunity.' So, it is with adversity. When the world hands you lemons, make lemonade, and remember that we are never alone if we have faith and remember that we are given particular tests and challenges we personally need for our eternal salvation and exaltation. This life was never intended to be easy, and our lives are made up of thousands of every day choices. Over the years these little choices will be bundled together and show clearly what we value. The crucial test of life does not revolve around who has the most money, the fanciest house, or this shiniest car. The greatest decision in life is between good and evil. We must always strive to stay on the Lord's side."

"Nothing makes any of us immune from the ravages of evil, of sickness, of financial reversals, or even of death. But I do know that it is often when we are in the darkest, most dire of straits, that we grow the most, and for this reason, adversity does have a place in our lives."

"Count your blessings, not your problems."

"Spirits are eternal. At the first organization in heaven we were all present, and saw the Savior chosen and appointed, and the plan of salvation made, and we sanctioned it. We are God's literal offspring. We were spirit children; He was glorified and exalted in the life that went before this one. We could tell the difference between our spirit bodies and the glorified and exalted body which he possessed. He taught us eternal truths; there came into our hearts the great desire to progress and advance and become like Him so that we could have glorified and exalted bodies and so that we could live in the family unit as He lived in the family unit. And consequently, He ordained and established what is called the Plan of Salvation."

"There is no place anywhere on this earth where you can be closer to Heaven than within the walls of the temple. You can check your concerns of the temporal world as the door and find peace and perspective in the House of the Lord. There is no place that I would rather be than in the tranquility of the temple."

"Death is a necessary part of God's plan for all of us, and for the salvation of all His people. We came into this world to acquire knowledge, to be tested, and then to die. That was understood long before we came here. It is part of the plan, all discussed and arranged long before men were placed on the Earth. When Adam was sent into this world, it was with the understanding that he would violate a law, transgress a law, learning that all things have their opposite, good and evil, virtue and vice, pleasure and pain, doing all this in order to bring about the mortal condition in which we find ourselves today."

"There is no place anywhere on this earth where you can be closer to Heaven than within the walls of the temple. You can check your concerns of the temporal world as the door and find peace and perspective in the House of the Lord. There is no place that I would rather be than in the tranquility of the temple."

"I have seen too many miracles to ever doubt that they occur."

"Now we do not seek death, though it is part of the merciful plan of the great Creator. Rather, we rejoice in life, and desire to live as long as we can be of service to our families and fellow me, striving to be beacons of righteousness in a wicked world. Some are chosen to linger and to suffer, in both body and spirit, to prove them in all things, and to see if they will abide in His covenant, even unto death, that they may be found worthy of eternal life."

"What would the world be like if we didn't have faith and the knowledge that miracles are possible because of faith. Faith always precedes the miracle."

"A simple act on our part can very well be a miracle in the life of another."

"The average twelve year old would probably want to go to Disneyland given the opportunity to make a wish; we were introduced to a young lady who wanted something much different. She wanted to meet the Lord's living prophet on the earth today and to talk to him about what Heaven is like. Unlike most of her twelve year old peers, Lydia Terry is dying of a rare form of brain cancer. My only question is: Why?"

"When all else fails, and the odds are against you, pray mightily, and remember that someone has to be in that special one percent."

"Miracle… defying logic, physical laws of science or nature…but nonetheless happening."

"How we are living in this world needs to be subservient to our ultimate destination."

"We need to be less rigid in our own personal spiritual development."

"There is a big difference between being a member of the Church and truly living the principles of the Gospel."

"We are here to be an influence on the world around us, and not to be influenced by the world."

"Satan is subtle; he won't pick up this building and move it across the street. What he will do is tempt you by inches until one day you are embroiled in sin. The key is to be forewarned and forearmed…and when all else fails, there is the Doctrine of Repentance available to enable you to start anew."

Goals & Work

"The brain is a goal seeking mechanism that deals in absolute values. Fill it with negative thoughts and you will subject yourself to self-fulfilled prophecies of failure and regret. On the other hand, fill your heart and mind with positive thoughts associated with the dreams of possibility, and you will experience success beyond your dreams."

"Sometimes the reward is not in the goal achieved,
but rather in the journey along the way."

"Never accept doing the minimum as your standard."

"More people are hurt climbing *down* the mountain than climbing up. We must not lose sight of life after we have reached whatever summit we have set our eyes."

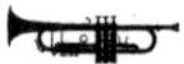

"If you aim for 60%, that is all you will achieve. I have always believed in shooting for 100%; whether I made it or not might depend on physical limitations, but in my heart, I was always a 100 percenter."

"Success at miniature golf, like most things in life, is all about staying focused on the objective, and being able to putt straight."

"I have never been satisfied with the status quo."

"A constant commitment to learning is how our minds stay agile and we remain young."

"Don't be part of the problem, be part of the solution."

"Are we investing our time in things that matter or are we merely spending our time in pursuits that are wasteful or slothful?"

"Ninety percent of our business is belief; the other half is activity. Plan to work, and then work the plan."

"Half empty, half full. You will be right half the time, depending on your attitude."

"Goals are nothing more than dreams with a deadline."

"Without goals, life is meaningless."

"One of the most exciting things about Life is knowing that we can always set additional goals to pursue and to achieve."

"Goals should stretch you, challenge you, and mean that much more when you finally achieve them."

"There will be times when we won't achieve our goals, and they are intended solely to make us better and to propel us further towards our ultimate objective."

Gratitude

"It is all about living life with an attitude of gratitude."

"You can't be grateful and greedy at the same time. They are mutually exclusive of one another."

"Always start your prayers with a list of things for which you are grateful."

"Generosity is a state of being or of mind, whereas charity is a state of action."

"Gratitude makes sense of our past, brings peace for today, and creates a vision for tomorrow."

"Gratitude should not be a concept that we only talk about over the Thanksgiving turkey and trimmings. It should be an ever present mindset and attitude."

"Another reason to always live with an attitude of gratitude is that there is scientific proof that living with an attitude of gratitude is actually a way to improve both mind and body. Don't believe it, well consider that studies have shown that this Attitude of gratitude has been proven to provide improved sleep (we can all use this), ease depression (you can't be grateful and sad at the same time), boosts immunity (I suspect that this is as much a case of mind over matter) and lowering stress (with ancillary high blood pressure and related maladies)."

"I'm just happier when I am grateful!"

"An attitude of gratitude can actually serve as an armor plated lifeline against all the negativity that we encounter every day."

"Gratitude is a set of blinders that we can wear to keep us safe against the blinding effects of sadness and the Adversary."

"It is better to live with a heart full of gratitude than full of regrets."

Happiness

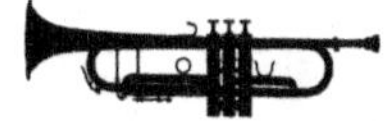

"We truly do control our own happiness. I am sorry to say that it has taken me nearly half my life to realize this basic truth."

"Fear does not come from the Lord.
Faith and Peace are fruits of the Spirit.
Satan attempts to bring out the darkness that is contained in all of us.
The key to happiness is to always strive for the light."

"Happiness is an awareness of all the positives that you have achieved in life and deriving satisfaction from it. It is not about mediocrity or missed opportunities but rather all about being grateful."

"Happiness is not a state to arrive at, but rather a manner of traveling."

"The key to happiness is maintaining an eternal perspective."

Happiness is…

“sharing a common bond with each of your children.”

“an unsaid expression of love that passes between you as she glances back over her shoulder as she walks into school, knowing that you will be there, the car not moving, until she gets safely inside, no matter how old she is getting.”

“Playing Santa for the umpteenth time.”

“watching your kids overcome their fears…”

"watching them walk at commencement with a countless array of tassels, ribbons, and other awards recognizing graduation."

"watching your kid master the high dive for the first time and taking that big plunge."

"watching them buy their first car or walking through the house that they are building."

"watching your child sleep from the doorway of their bedroom."

"listening to that pre-teen sing off key"

"chocolate kisses on the cheek."

"watching that first drive, or that first hole-in-one, and knowing that you couldn't have done any better."

"watching your child master the intricacies of a child-proof medicine cap."

"watching your child run to school with a knapsack filled with books, treasures, and the mysteries of the universe on his or her back."

"Having your nearly 11 year old child stand up for her principles, and not knuckling under to peer pressure to do something that she believes to be fundamentally wrong."

"being able to detect the formation of adult features in the faces of your children."

"watching your son clear the bases with a deep drive over the outfielders' heads."

"watching your son stick his vault."

"participating in your missionary's farewell."

"participating in your son's Eagle Court of Honor."

"participating in your daughter's Young Womanhood Recognition."

"when your child displays a talent, you yourself don't possess."

"the dance recital..."

"watching your grandson masterfully employ
scissors to the newspaper."

"watching your own child or grandchild grasp the
concept of responsibility for self, for education, for
testimony, and for their own achievements."

"the rock and paper stand that often replaced
the sidewalk lemonade stand."

"holding that newborn grandchild for the first time."

"receiving ALL the first day of school pictures for each grandchild as they embark on the next year's adventures."

"realizing that you are the linkage between your grandparents and your grandchildren."

"knock, knock jokes."

"when they start displaying their own sense of humor. Even better, when they laugh at Grandpa's jokes."

"receiving unexpected assistance with raking the leaves."

"Halloween trick or treating"

"I miss you much…"

"sharing the joy of one of the children taking firm hold of the next challenge in his life and embracing with enthusiasm acceptance into the doctoral program."

"Green gum."

"learning that the first person of the next generation is on her way...becoming a great-grandparent for the first time."

"still being genuinely excited over the most recent [grand] baby's latest weight check at the doctor's office."

"Night, love you, same."

"Life talks."

"giving someone a gift that becomes their prized possession."

"tickets for Spring Training baseball with a good friend."

"being told that you are trust more than anyone else."

"seeing *Mary Poppins, Feed the Birds* (Tuppence a Bag) embraced by the next generation."

"Feeling that new grandbaby kicking away
in your own baby's tummy!"

"When we are the recipients of a delicious home cooked meal from one of the kids because Mom is not feeling well."

"Don't rely on others to make you happy. Be happy when you wake up and realize that you have the gift of another day with those you love."

"Grandpa always smells good… he has bubble gum!"

"Oh, I always wanted that. What is it?"

"And the cold wind blew…."

"Bootch!"

"Beam me up Scotty on the waterbed…"

"Chocolate Crinkles at Christmas."

"I love you more than a million red M&Ms."

Honor & Integrity

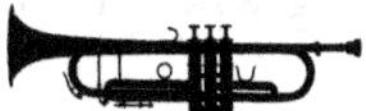

"Ethics is more than just knowing what to do in a given situation – it is all about having the courage to ACT, even when it may make you unpopular, threatens your position, or runs contrary to the party line. In terms of teaching our children, it simply is doing what's right even when no one else is looking."

"We always have to be mindful of our own True North."

"God, Family, Honor, Duty, Country – is there anything more?"

"Compromise is always wrong when it means sacrificing a principle."

"The beauty of integrity and ethics is that it is very black and white. There is no gray. Gray is merely a shade of black. As a former leader shared with me, "you can't be a little pregnant. Either you are or you are not." So it is with ethics and integrity. Either we possess them, or we don't. There is no such thing as situational ethics. This is nothing more than rationalization which is the single greatest means by which we find ourselves on the proverbial slippery slope."

"In my mind, the greatest sin we can create in this world is to die without honor."

"We lost a giant of a man when John McCain passed away just shy of his 82nd birthday. While he will be remembered as a maverick and a warrior of the United States Senate, I think it is equally important to remember that he was a Prisoner of War in Vietnam's infamous 'Hanoi Hilton' for over six and one-half years, having refused early release solely because he was the son of a [four-star] Admiral who was Commander, United States Pacific Command and then commander of all U.S. forces in the Vietnam theatre. When he was shot down, McCain broke both arms, a leg, and suffered other injuries. During his imprisonment he was denied need medical treatment and subjected to years of torture by the North Vietnamese. He spent much of his time as a POW in solitary confinement, but never broke. John McCain was a tenacious soul, respected by members of both political parties because of his Honor and Integrity. These are attributes sorely lacking in the world today. I voted for him in 2008 when he was the Republican standard bearer for President of the United States."

"Remember who you are…"

"Death before Dishonor."

"We lost another giant of a man at the end of 2018. President George Herbert Walker Bush died at age 94, and when I shared the news with my wife, she gasped, and was immediately saddened. The last of the Greatest Generation. With a vita that included decorated U.S. Navy fighter pilot during World War II, businessman, entrepreneur, Congressman, Ambassador to China, Ambassador to the United Nations, Director of the CIA, Vice President of the United States, and finally the 41st President of the United States, I can't think of a man who was more *qualified* for office when he became president on January 20, 1989. Of even greater significance however was the manner in which he served our country as a man guided by honor and integrity. Regardless of where and how he was called upon to serve, he did so faithfully and honorably. I have been astounded by the heartfelt tributes from former U.S. Presidents from both political parties, world leaders, but most importantly from his children and grandchildren who all remember him as a giant of a man. He was President when the Berlin Wall came down, for the reunification of Germany, a wartime president during the first Persian Gulf War, and other historical events. More history again during my lifetime. I have every confidence that History will judge him one of our better presidents. Rest in Peace 41."

"Music is intended to elicit emotional responses from us. Some of them happy, others sad. The stirring sounds of a spirited John Philip Sousa march to the melancholy strains of Nearer My God to Thee. Combining them in a state funeral is nearly enough to do me in."

"Is there anything more mournful, more evident of sacrifice, than the ritual precision of a military funeral. As is usually the case, I could only watch the final tribute to President George H. W. Bush as his earthly remains were removed down the steps of the U.S. Capitol building, where he had lain in state for the past two days, by the Honor Guard of select uniformed military personnel, through tear-filled eyes.

The government is closed today; the stock markets are closed as well, there won't be any mail delivery, as we all collectively pause to remember this good and decent man. 'Good and decent' – not words we hear too often when associated with the politicians who we choose to lead us. The number of foreign dignitaries and world leaders gathered in the National Cathedral is further testimony of the difference one person can make in this world.

Part of the Greatest Generation, it was amazing to watch former Senator Bob Dole, 95 years of age, confined to a wheelchair, being wheeled to the side of President Bush's flag-draped coffin, assisted to his feet by an aide, and his rendering a salute with an arthritically deformed left hand (his right arm having been rendered useless in WWII combat) in final tribute to his fellow warrior.

From some of President Bush's final comments, he did not fear death, and was secure in the knowledge that he would now be reunited with his wife of seventy-three years and their daughter who died at age four from childhood leukemia. Can there be any doubt of the eternal perspective everyone, even if only privately or secretly, clings to in hopes of remaining with their loved ones? His last words: 'I love you too.'"

"As I reflect on history, I remember as a five year old child being amazed that all THREE of the network channels broadcast images of President Kennedy's casket from the Rotunda of the U.S. Capitol. In my memories it seems that there was nothing else being broadcast. That was a devastating time in our Nation's history. I do remember the profound sadness that it put in everyone's heart.

In recent times I can recall the funerals of Lyndon Johnson, Richard Nixon, Gerald Ford, and Ronald Reagan, and while the pageantry was largely the same, I did not feel the same as I did watching the earthly remains of George H.W. Bush being reverently moved by his honor guard. I guess that is because in Bush 41 I actually lost a personal hero who personified the best of Honor and Integrity."

"It still strikes me as nothing short of amazing that after losing to Bill Clinton in the 1992 election and being denied a second term in office, circumstances allowed these two men to become more than just good friends. In a lot of ways Bush 41 became the father that Bill Clinton never had. Regaled as part of the Bush family, it was easy to see what the passing of George Bush meant to Bill Clinton."

"The flag is at half-mast on the flagpole next to our driveway. I saw many flags at half-mast in my travels today. Upon reflection, it is nothing short of amazing how lowering the flag to half-mast conveys so much. It is symbolic of the collective loss we have suffered as a nation as well as paying a tribute from a grateful nation."

"I can remember the number of times that I stood on the [artillery] gun line, giving orders to fire, and taking a certain pride in the raw power as the large rounds left the tubes and streaked across the sky ready to impact on their intended targets. It is amazing how mournful those small 105mm powder-charge-only volleys can sound to me as they pay tribute to a fallen leader."

"The flag draped coffin is the ultimate reminder of honorable service and sacrifice."

"We all wonder what people will say about us after we depart this world. Instead of wondering, live the life that portrays what you want them to say."

"Actions really do speak louder than words. Live a life of honor, integrity, and loyalty, and allow your deeds to have the final word."

Joy & Kindness

"No doubt about it, but charity and generosity really are gifts that we give to ourselves."

"Work was not intended as a punishment or a chore, but rather a passion to be explored and cultivated."

"There is much joy to be found in the service to others less fortunate than ourselves."

"We are responsible for finding our own Joy. You will never be handed happiness and joy, you make it."

"Nobody can take the joy from our lives unless we willingly surrender it."

"With each passing year and entry into the next phase of my life, I continue to learn the significance of the adage that indicates the importance of finding joy in the journey, for it is truly not a destination unto itself."

"Every day we have a choice. We can either be a voice for all that is right in the world or take the negative road. One brings satisfaction; the other nothing but unhappiness."

"What I have discovered after all these years is the importance of living in the moment and simply enjoying every minute of Today. You can't spend all of your days waiting for better ones ahead because if you are not where you are, you are nowhere."

"There can actually be quite a bit of joy found in the routine things of life. The key to finding them is the attitude with which we approach them."

"Find joy in the innocence of your grandchildren. Their first words, first steps, first acts of independence. For as soon as they come, these firsts are forever gone."

"On a daily basis, we should all strive to make the difference in the life of another person. Doing this, seemingly for their benefit, will only bring greater joy to our own lives."

"Find joy even in your smallest acts of kindness."

"There is joy in everything around us if we look deeply enough."

"Sometimes you can derive joy from simply being able to do the little things that we often take for granted."

"Kindness is more important than all of the wisdom or wealth that we can accumulate in a lifetime."

"Try to perform one random act of kindness each day. You will be better for it."

"Think of kindness as a candle; you will lose nothing by lighting the flame of another's candle."

"Like the certainty of a mathematical equation, there is no way to brighten another person's life with an act of kindness with the reciprocal value being added to your own."

"An act of kindness is not a sign of weakness but rather the ultimate manifestation of strength."

"A kind word for a troubled ear may be short in nature but can live on for eternity in the heart of the recipient."

"I suspect that we will often be remembered for our small acts of kindness rather than for our acts of achievement."

"How different would our world be if it was always filled with the kindness that is exhibited in the name of charity during the holiday season?"

"When General Ulysses S. Grant accepted General Robert E. Lee's surrender of the Army of Northern Virginia, he did more to promote post-war peace with simple acts of respect and kindness than anything else at his disposal."

"With every act of kindness, you share a tiny piece of yourself."

"Sometimes it is simply left to us to cultivate a feeling of joy when encountering unexplainable trials."

"The Gospel and its inherent truth should be a joy in all of our lives."

LEADERSHIP

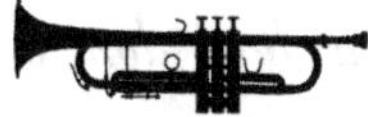

"It has been said that it is 'lonely at the top.' That leadership is all about loneliness and shouldering the responsibility of defeat and the sharing of the credit for success. I suspect that the price of true leadership may entail an element of loneliness by design. True leadership requires unflagging adherence to our principles and the character of our souls. Whether at work, at home, or at play, the leader must endure and persevere especially in the face of adversity and tough decisions. To do otherwise is to relinquish the guidon of command."

"The mark of any command or leadership tenure is to leave the organization better than when you found it."

"For many years, I wore a pewter starfish in the lapel of my suit. I wore it to remind myself of the parable of the starfish but also to incite people to ask me about it, thus allowing to share with them the story of the starfish. *After a huge storm, a man walked alone on a beach where thousands of starfish had been washed up onto the sand far from the water's edge. In the distance, he saw a young boy bending to grab something, then straightening up, and with great effort, hurling something into the sea. When the man grew closer and could observe what the boy was doing, he saw that he was gathering starfish, one by one, and returning them back to the sea. The man asked the boy what he thought he was doing. "If these starfish don't get back into the water, they will surely die," said the boy. "But there are thousands of starfish on this beach," said the man. What possible difference can it make?" "To this one," answered the boy as he gazed at the starfish he was holding in his hand, "it makes all the difference in the world." Live your life so as to always make all the difference in the world to the person or organization that you are serving."*

"As leaders, our role is to keep one eye in the rearview mirror so as to be conscious of where we have come from, but more importantly to keep our eyes on the road ahead as well as the horizon."

Things that I have learned on temperament and relationships… and the art of command and leadership:

"Keep a tight rein on your temper."

"'Controlled anger' can be a very powerful tool if is only broken out on rare occasion."

"Don't let your mouth overload your brain…or your brawn."

"If you want to be respected, be respectful of others."

"Learn to say, 'I'm sorry' and 'I'm wrong' – not just 'you're right' – people will respect you more, listen with greater attention, and be more apt to follow you."

"Leave everything a little better than you found it. If it is entrusted to you, treat it as your own, and strive to make it better."

"A man's word is his bond – without it, he is nothing."

"Don't take sunshine and natural beauty for granted."

"Leadership is not limited to those who seemingly are imbued with it naturally. It can also be learned. What it really comes down to is a concern for the people we are charged with leading."

"Loyalty is a two way street that requires giving as well as taking."

"If you want 1 year of prosperity, grow rice.
If you want 10 years of prosperity, grow trees.
If you want 100 years of prosperity, grow people."
-Chinese Proverb
This particular proverb has graced the pages of nearly
every business plan that I have ever constructed.
DJL

"Everything in business, and Life for that
matter, is about relationships."

"When you are the leader, it's important to remember…
… Everyone is watching
… Everyone is listening
… What you say *really* matters.
… Consistency is the key.
… To say what you will do and do what you say."

"The best way to teach something is by example."

"As leaders, it us up to us to blaze the trail and
forge a path for our team to follow."

"As leaders it is up to us to always display calm under fire, to discover order in chaos, and to overcome our own personal limitations and fears. A great example of this is President John F. Kennedy's own wartime experience when leading the survivors of his *PT-109* after it had been sunk and rammed by a Japanese destroyer."

"Leaders accept responsibility for all that goes wrong, and shares credit for all that goes right."

"When overcome with too much business, too many opportunities, being stretched in too many ways, I have always professed that 'this is a good problem to have.'"

"Enthusiasm is the force multiplier that allows the rookie to outsell the veteran salesman; for the rookie to outhustle the veteran on the ballfield or court and is the quintessential element that is the difference between success and failure."

"Leaders keep one eye on the horizon, and one on the ground in front of them in order to spot speed bumps."

"Regardless of the endeavor or the product, no team, no company, no business, can ever better than its people or those who lead them."

"I have had many people take me to task for my optimism. I figure if that is the worst thing that they can call me on, I am okay with that; nobody wants to be with, much less follow, a negative leader."

"Years ago, when I was appointed a divisional vice president for sales, I was interviewed for the company newsletter and was asked what had prepared me the most for the journey as a DVP I was about to embark on. Many expected me to say my twenty three years of military service, or my time as a regional sales manager, when I believe it was the thirty some odd years of parenting. My role as a parent has not been to make all the right choices for my children but to teach them how to reason and to make proper choices for themselves. I believe the same can be said for agents and the ethical environment we establish for our agencies. Our role as leader is not all that different than that of parent: it is incumbent us to create a compass by which we can all live and operate, and to establish what true North is all about. For me, true North has always been about integrity. It is about living life as a role model; Kouzes and Posner refer to it as Modeling the Way."

"As leaders, our responsibility is not to *motivate* but to *inspire* our followers."

"It is hard to remember that your mission was to drain the swamp when you are up to your butt in alligators."

"If power corrupts, and absolute power corrupts absolutely, then we have to be cognitive of the corollary that the power to lead is also the power to mislead. As leaders it is incumbent upon us to always take the high road of integrity, because the power to mislead can also be the power of destruction. Whether as leaders of countries or companies, all too often this *power* has been the downfall of leader and followers alike. One only has to look at the rise and fall of Nazi Germany to recognize the veracity of this premise."

"Adopt true principles of integrity early in life and then adhere to them with total inflexibility. Followers, peers, and superiors will all respect you for it."

"There will always be times when you are the new guy. You may be replacing someone who was held in high esteem leaving large shoes to fill. Never disparage their memory or their accomplishments, and humble yourself enough to earn the trust and respect of those who are charged to lead."

"As the leader, you are charged with setting the tone and pace of the organization. It is important to remember that the organization will adopt your personality and way of doing things; therefore, be ready on the first day to set the tone, and to set the bar high. Personally, I have had this experience as a senior sales leader, Army unit commander, and lay leader of a religious congregation. For this reason, I know that this is a universal truth."

"Don't be afraid to cast your own shadow as a leader."

"As the leader, it is not necessary for us to always be centerstage. Some of the best leaders achieved the most results by exercising their *influence* from the wings of the stage."

"Always strive to create an environment – a culture – in which followers feel both comfortable and encouraged to speak their minds and to share opinions. This is a key ingredient to building consensus as a team and will quite often be the force multiplier that can be the difference between success and failure."

"Leaders must maintain an even keel. We are not allowed to 'explode' or to go off on tangents. Followers, whether in the home, office, or chain of command, will find both comfort and security in the consistency or constancy of the leader."

"Good leaders seek to influence…not dominate."

"Leadership roles can be assigned, but the mantel of true leadership has to be earned."

"Leaders recognize the talents of their followers and strive to allow these talents to be fully utilized. Morale is another one of those force multipliers that has to be cultivated and nourished."

"Leaders are responsible for linking short-term goals with long-term objectives."

"Leaders make the seemingly impossible possible by breaking down the long term objective into palatable short term bites."

"Leaders recognize that running the marathon requires a steady, even pace and completing the race one mile at a time, even one step at a time."

"Leaders are responsible for being the CRO – the Chief Reminding Officer – and insuring that everyone stays fully vested and mindful of the organization's *why* for existing."

"Leaders don't rely on others to achieve their vision. They are out in front, leading the charge, modeling the way, and always maintaining a path centered on True North."

"Leaders have to remain positive, focused, and prepared to make any sacrifice necessary to achieve the immediate results necessary to achieving the long term goal associated with organization's vision."

"It is up to the leader to keep his eye on the ball; to know where the puck is going, and to always be thinking at least three steps ahead."

"Leaders live their lives backwards. With an eye to where they and the organization needs or wants to be in five years, and the other eye looking backward to determine the milestones and strategies necessary to achieve these long term goals."

"Leaders are ultimately responsible for everything good and bad that happens within the organization regardless of how unlikely he or she may have personally influenced the ultimate result achieved. This responsibility may make you a hero one day and a dog the next. The key is to keep the highs from getting too high and the lows too low. Again, it is all about maintaining steadfastness in our words and deeds."

"All leaders need a place that they can go to and recharge their batteries. Superman had his Fortress of Solitude. Camp David was designed to afford our nation's leader the same refuge. Make sure that you find such a place for yourself."

"Adversity is the true test of leadership. How we respond to the unexpected and the challenging, will often dictate how our followers ultimately respond to our leadership."

"Years ago, I took over the last place agency in our company. My rationale is that there was no place to go but up. Conversely, after we had achieved the number one status, I realized that while we could devote our efforts to remaining number one, the odds [and the metrics by which we were ranked] would catch up with us, and the fall from number one was inevitable. The key to successful leadership is to recognize the integrity of this system."

"As leaders we are always being judged. The key is to never compromise our principles and undermine our authority to lead."

"Leaders have to always 'walk the walk' and not merely 'talk the talk.' For as certain as the sun will come up tomorrow morning, when a leader ceases to walk the walk, someone will come along to challenge him for this shortcoming."

"Leadership takes on many forms. It can require physical courage as in combat, emotional and intellectual courage to conquer personal fears, and moral courage to remain true to the faith as the keeper of visionary compass."

"Leaders understand the power associated with shared values and must work diligently in crafting the vision and making it palpable to his followers."

"Leaders are always training and developing their successors."

"Good leaders always strive to be mentors to those following them. Attaining the status and recognition as a Leader-Coach should be the ultimate goal of every leader."

"Leaders want to surround themselves with people smarter than themselves."

"Even champion-caliber players and team members will come in second or fail to make that winning shot. As leaders, you want to stock your team with players who are over achievers and highly competitive BUT can handle the occasional disappointment with dignity and grace, and renewed commitment to winning and achievement."

"As a leader it is of paramount importance that you do not over react in the face of adversity and that you are able to maintain the proper perspective."

"Good leaders can help their followers achieve extraordinary goals. By crafting a vision with vivid imagery and creating an environment in which people can feel part of something larger than themselves, they will go the extra mile and become part of the larger solution. I can remember one instance when we were engaged in a 'fire sale' of a product that was being closed out. At that time, our usual production was approximately $125,000 per week. Our hope was that with the proper *inspiration* that the team could achieve sales of approximately $250-300,000. Imagine my surprise when the final tally was over $605,000. It was even more gratifying when several members of the team said that they were able to far exceed their own personal goals because of the steady stream of recognition, enthusiasm and *encouragement* that they received from me in the form of group voice mails, texts, and e-mails several times per day. As a sales leader, it was probably the greatest week that I ever experienced. What made it so great is that EVERYONE contributed, and we left nobody behind in the winner's circle."

"Never confuse inspiration and motivation. They are totally different things. One is your responsibility as the leader, the other the responsibility of the follower."

"You can't be a successful leader unless you know what you stand for, and more importantly, your followers have this same knowledge."

"As the leader, it is important that you always know what direction you are going in; never lose sight of the compass. The people behind you are depending on you."

"In the 1980s, the Chicago Bulls were an up and coming team. Michael Jordan joined the team and a metamorphosis occurred. Fifty win seasons became a regular thing, as did the playoffs, but the Detroit Pistons seemed to be an immovable road block to the Bulls in the playoffs. And then it happened. Beliefs made things happen for the Bulls, and it started with their leaders; Phil Jackson behind the bench, and Michael Jordan on the floor. The rest we say is history."

"As leaders, it is important for us to ensure that everyone on the team knows the short term and intermediate objectives, as well as the long term goal."

"As a sales leader we attempt to keep the team in check and to avoid the higher highs and lower lows. The rule in our agency was that on Friday and Saturday we would either celebrate or commiserate over the previous week's sales figures, but come Monday, it was a new week, and we had to start at zero all over again in hopes of making it another winning week. Because in sales, you really are only as good as your last sale!"

"In our business we are always talking about the passion and the zeal of a missionary with which we talk to our clients. As leaders it is our responsibility to ensure that our mission and our vision statements mirror this passion and serve as a reminder of the Why we are doing what we do each and every day."

"You can't lead from your desk. Transformational leadership requires you to be in the trenches, leading by example, modeling the way, and demonstrating your competence on a regular basis."

"As leaders and parents, it is absolutely critical that we observe and acknowledge when our followers or children do what they are supposed to do, e.g. have the requisite number of appointments scheduled or complete their homework without being badgered."

"I learned years ago, from a fellow leader whom I respect immensely, 'that agents will do for love what they won't do for money.' By this she meant that positive consequences such as awards, recognition, incentives can have a HUGE impact on the organization's achieving its collective goals."

"Don't confuse doing those things that are *urgent* with those things that are *important.* It is all about the people."

"Never forget the importance of the 'Love Sandwich.' If you must correct a mistake, reprimand a behavior, or simply re-direct focus and effort, remember to begin, and end, with an expression of concern for the individual. It is all about *demonstrating* that you value them as a person."

"Good leaders are humble and recognize that they must continue to grow and learn themselves from those around them."
Wisdom of the Diamond

LIFE LESSONS

"Can the wisdom of 'measure twice, cut once,' ever be overstated? It is a rule that has resonated with, and guided me, in every aspect of my life. It is a lesson that I have unfortunately had to learn more than once."

"My maternal grandfather spent his entire adult life selling children's shoes. He taught me never to buy cheap shoes – only leather will ever do, and to polish them before you wear them for the first time. The polish will protect the leather from scuffs and cuts and contribute to a longer life for the shoes."

"I remain astounded at how powerful the use of 'sir' and 'ma'am' as well as 'please' and 'thank you' remain in today's Society."

"Hold the door at a store and be surprised at the reaction of the person to whom you have just extended this courtesy."

"With all the shoes and boots that I polished in the course of twenty six years of military service, the greatest luxury I can afford myself is that of a shoeshine at the airport. Even better is the complimentary shoe shine provided by many luxury hotels. Free is always better."

"It is important to take care of the shine of your shoes because you will often be judged solely on their appearance."

"Your feet will carry you places but only if you take care of them as you expect them to take care of you."

"Your smile can convey so much about you. Take care of your teeth, you only get one set to keep. Contrary to what you may hear, flossing is important."

"I remain convinced that the best way to
learn something is to teach it."

"I waited a lot of years, but owning a convertible is definitely the way to go if you want to really feel alive while you are driving."

"The best way to get through life is to laugh your way through it."

"Never underestimate the power of a handwritten note especially in this day and age of e-mail, twitter, and other forms of social media."

"Don't take yourself too seriously…"

"Don't concern yourself with learning the shortcuts or relying on cheat sheets, simply learn the trade in which you are engaged in better than anyone else."

"Don't be quick to blame others when things don't go your way. Take responsibility for all aspects of your life."

"If you ever encounter a disruptive influence in your class while teaching, invite said disruptive force to in turn teach the next class. The lesson he will learn is that one cannot be the ringmaster and clown in the circus at the same time."

"Calling servers, store clerks, and other service providers wearing a name tag by their first name is a way to show appreciation for them and to share a little kindness."

"Open your mind by reading. Books have the power to take you places that you may only visit in your dreams."

"Don't be part of the problem. Be part of the solution."

"It took me until I was forty eight years old to realize that 95% of the bad stuff that I worried about never came to fruition. It was a waste of my time, effort, and energy. Life is better when you don't worry."

"You can't hire someone to work out for you."

"Discovered answers will resonate with greater truth."

"While often elusive, when finally possessed, Patience strengthens the spirit, sweetens the temper, stifles anger, subdues pride, opens the heart, and bridles the tongue."

"Listening is an art form that requires more than just your ears."
DJL June 1995

"The only person that I need to be better than
today is the person I was yesterday."

"Practice does not make perfect. Perfect Practice makes perfect."

"Temper gets people into trouble, but pride keeps them there."

"Pride is a foolish man's luxury often ill-afforded."

"Tell the truth, and there is less to remember."

"The truly great man learns the lessons that accompany disappointments, failures, and the trials and tribulations that we encounter along our journey through life."

"Never underestimate the power of a simple platonic hug."

"Watching is an important part of listening. It is tone, pace, and body language that often makes the difference between communicating and miscommunicating."

"Stay grounded. Watch *It's A Wonderful Life* at least once during every Christmas season. It is a great way to put things in perspective."

"Never allow your actions to be fueled by vengeance or spite for it will surely boomerang on you."

"If you are walking away from something, don't look back."

"When you encounter a drowning man, that is not the time to attempt to teach him how to swim. Throw him a life preserver first."

"A single idea has the ability to change a life or even the world."

"New ideas don't come from maintaining the status quo. It is all about thinking outside the box."
"Inside of every disaster is an opportunity waiting to be discovered."

"I am constantly amazed at how often people will use words and phrases without knowing the full import of these words. For the record, a literal **goat rope** is an activity at a fair where many people try to catch goats with a rope. Obviously, this would be very chaotic and unorganized. This **expression** first started appearing in the 1900s. We sometimes use it to describe our family get togethers."

"We are never too old to learn from those who have greater wisdom than ourselves. I will be forever grateful to dear friends and mentors who continue to see a greater light within me than I sometimes can discern on my own."

."As we go through our mortal sojourn, one of the greatest skills we must master is the ability to discern between that which is truly important and those things that are insignificant. Put another way, we must stop 'majoring in the minors' and avoid getting lost in the weeds. All too often I will speak to people who find it necessary to tell me how to build the clock when all I am interested in at that moment is the time."

"If we are receptive, we can learn lessons in just about any experience of life, even attending the theatre. I remember being dragged to a Shakespeare festival and wondering why the man could not write plays in which the actors were able to speak in plain English. And what of opera, and musicals? Much like a computer where it is easy to understand the concept of 'garbage in, garbage out,' it is about the effort we put into *understanding* the message that is being shared. I took this lesson away from a viewing of *Camelot.* Honestly, I don't remember very much, I may very well have dozed through some of the high school performance that I was attending, but I do remember a lesson I learned that night some forty plus years ago from King Arthur: 'violence is not strength, and compassion is not weakness.' That simple line resonated in the heart of a sixteen year old about to begin college and continues to do so to this day."

"Never underestimate the joy or value of reading. I read recently that fully one-third of all Americans with college degrees did not read a single book in the previous year. I can't imagine it. I read between 50-60 books of all genres on an annual basis. I read for pleasure, to expand my mind, and to continue my pursuit of knowledge. Read the Scriptures, read about history – or you will soon forget it, read the classics – broaden your mind, read the newspaper to stay abreast of the world around you, and remember that when you have a book with you, you are never alone."

"Have you noticed how illiterate our younger generation sounds with their choice of syntax? That reading aloud, much less public speaking, is a real challenge for them? I attribute this to the lack of reading and writing that accompanies the use of texting. OMG! IMO this will be the downfall of civilization."

"It is truly a big world out there. Full of mystery and wonder. Come out of your electronic and virtual devices and EXPERIENCE life."

"From time to time we all need a reminder to heed the words of Michael Swift, 'may you live all the days of your life.' I suspect that many of us will squander a great deal of our God-given finite time in less than fruitful pursuits."

"We were all put here to be participants in life... not observers. Get involved, make a difference, but do something!"

"I simply love history. It has been a passion of mine from the time that I was a child. I fear that less and less people, particularly our children and grandchildren, have even an inkling of the importance of reading about and embracing it, particularly while charting a course for themselves and their families. The late Daniel Boorstin (who is he you ask), a past Librarian of Congress (that's who), said that trying to plan for the future without an eye to the past is like trying to plant cut flowers. Think about that image for a second, because we all know that you simply cannot plant cut flowers. They will not take root and will simply wither and die. It is up to us 'older folks' to make history interesting and to come alive."

"Make history come alive you say? How does one do that? Well, a couple of years ago I spoke to my granddaughter's second grade class (actually all four second grade classes) about the Civil War. I brought with me musket balls harvested from the battlefield at Gettysburg, a replica of a Civil War era uniform, and even tried my hand at baking hardtack. Nearly one hundred kids were engaged that day, and I felt like maybe, just maybe, I had planted some seeds. The day was deemed a success. Fast forward three years, and amidst my family history research, I learned that we had not one, not two, but at least three ancestors who fought on the side of the Confederacy. Captain Jacob Cohen died at the Battle of Manassas, and is buried in the Hebrew National Cemetery in Richmond, VA.

Major Alexander Hart, founder of the Temple House of Israel in Staunton, VA participated in the Battle of Chancellorsville with Major General Jubal Early's division. He received a serious leg injury at the Battle of Antietam. He was taken to a private house after the battle. The surgeon said that the leg had to be amputated. The lady of the house begged the surgeon to wait and give her a chance to nurse Alexander back to health, proclaiming, 'So young and handsome a man should not lose a leg.' She did indeed nurse him back to health, and after the war, Major Hart visited his friend every year. Major Hart was on medical leave for five months, returned to participate in the Chancellorsville campaign, was injured again at Gettysburg, and certified as permanently disabled. However, he demanded a review, and rejoined his regiment to participate in the battle of Kernstown. He was captured in the third battle of Winchester and released through a prisoner-of-war exchange.

After the war, Major Hart went to Richmond, where he married Leonora Levy and went into the dry goods business with her family. Later, Major and Mrs. Hart moved to Staunton, where he was the founder and first president of Temple House of Israel in 1876. He was elected president and held that position for eighteen years.

Major Hart was active in the Confederate War Veterans, serving as a commander in the Pickett-Buchanan Camp in Norfolk after relocating there later in life. He was reported to have led services at the Ohef Shalom temple there when the rabbi was absent. He died in Norfolk in 1911 just ten days shy of his 72nd birthday and was buried there. His ceremonial sword is now on display at the National Museum of American Jewish History in Philadelphia, PA.

As noted, I discovered Major Hart, my first cousin four times removed, as well as all the above information, while in the course of my family history research. Imagine my joy when I even found a picture of him in his military uniform. When I was able to show my grandchildren who had been in the classroom three years ago for my Civil War lesson, an actual picture of their ancestor – putting a face to the name– and share these facts with them, the gleam in their eyes was payment enough as we connected with a family figure who certainly made a difference in the world around him some one hundred and fifty years ago, and made History come alive and more importantly, relevant to those of us alive today."

"I love reading David McCullough's accounts of history. From his biographies of John Adams and Harry Truman to accounts of the building of the Brooklyn Bridge and the Panama Canal, he is the quintessential historical storyteller. He makes history come alive for the reader. The key to his success is that he teaches us about history by emulating another great historian and writer Barbara Tuchman. Ms. Tuchman wrote the classic *The Guns of August* about World War I and summed up the teaching of history in two words: 'Tell stories.' I am flattered that people have labeled me with the moniker of 'story teller,' and hope that the stories don't become too repetitive. For those who may have heard them more than once, I apologize…again."

"I am constantly reminded of the fragility of the human body. A healthy body is something not to be taken for granted. High blood pressure, dreaded cancer, and the eventual and unavoidable frailties associated with advancing age certainly makes getting older a sobering event. In other words, getting older is not for sissies."

"Even with a workbench full of tools, the very best and my favorite tool is still my index finger. Whether it is smoothing caulk in between tile, or repairing cracks on the driveway with liquid cement, no tool quite possesses the versatility and accuracy of an index finger. My one fear is that I am going to wear it out."

"Life is best when you no longer have an agenda to prove but merely to live."

"Be a better listener than a talker."

"People need to be reminded that they are important. Encouraging the heart is not only a gift that we exercise for the good of the organization, but also of the individual. We all need to be validated and made to feel that our opinions and actions do make a difference."

"Simplicity is the ultimate sophistication."
"When all else fails, pull out the directions.
It can often be a time-saver."

"Experiencing life and asking questions are
the best ways to grow as a person."

"I always feel better when the sun comes out from behind the clouds. No matter what the rest of the day has been like, the warming touch of the sun is magical."

"If you find something that you are good at, that you enjoy doing, and can make a decent living doing it, then stick with it. Don't be swayed by what other people may say or be tempted to chase the next brass ring and potentially higher salary."

"Don't burn bridges by alienating people, particularly in the work environment. You never know when you may be seeing that person pop up in your sphere of influence."

"Years ago, I was in a situation to sit for three rather rigorous exams with a passing score of 70 BUT very high failure rates. As it was, I earned a 76 on my first attempt at each exam. Many of my peers joked that I had over prepared. I am here to tell you that there is no such thing as over preparation."

"For the years that I was on active duty with the U.S. Army, I was grateful that we were largely discouraged from talking politics and religion, and other 'controversial' topics. In this day and age, it is even more important to avoid these topics as well as other sensitive topics in the workplace. Once the words are out of your mouth, they are out there forever."

"If you or one of your subordinates or children make a mistake, simply own it. Don't try to pass on the blame or make an excuse. Own it and learn from it. If in fact it is a mistake on the part of one of your subordinates or children, don't badger them, but rather step up gently as a mentor and help them learn from their errors. Rubbing their noise in it or publicly berating them to the point of humiliation will never provide a satisfactory outcome."

"You can't want it – whatever 'it' is – more than the person you are leading or coaching. They have to want it too!"

"Vacations are an absolute must if you want to remain effective in whatever endeavor in which you are engaged. I was 32 years old before I took my first 'adult' vacation. I always thought that if I was not working that I was not making money and doing right by family. Wrong!"

"Don't make snap decisions or hasty judgments. Make sure that you take the time to gather the facts and weigh them appropriately. That is not to say become a procrastinator or fail to make decisions in a timely manner, but don't get into the habit of 'knee jerk' management. Sooner or later it is going to come back and bite you squarely on the backside."

"Bad news never gets better with age. If you have the dubious distinction of delivering, much less owning, it, do it quickly."

"When you lose respect for your boss and/or the organization, it is time to find the door, and another opportunity."

"'Because I said so' may work with young children but should be avoided in the workplace at all costs. Subordinates who are bullied by their leaders will never perform at the level desired by the organization. 'Pulling rank' is not influence or leadership but merely autocracy."

"There is a fine line between bold and brash. The key is to know where that line is and not to inadvertently cross over it."

"It is important to focus on the task at hand and to give it a no-holds-barred effort through to completion. However, it is equally important not to become so obsessed with completing one task that you allow other goals and responsibilities to fall by the wayside."

"A good negotiation occurs when both sides leave the table a little unhappy. If one party is happy while the other miserable, that is not a good negotiation session."

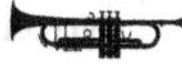

"If you ever find yourself in a position to have to negotiate, better to do it from a position of strength and remembering that 'he who speaks first often loses.' Always resist the temptation to speak first, and if possible, force the other side to make the first offer."

"As a young lieutenant, I accidentally learned a valuable lesson. By assisting my troops erect the multi-piece masted antenna with its various and sundry guide lines as well as the camouflage nets, I earned their respect by demonstrating a willingness to get my hands dirty alongside them, especially when the chips were down, and time was of the essence."

"If you have a 'clown' in your organization, make him the ringmaster for a day. You simply cannot be the clown and the ringmaster of the circus at the same time. I quite often would take a disruptive teenager from a class and make him the teacher for the day. It never ceased to amaze me the metamorphosis that occurred in him."

"It is up to us to cultivate our talents to the best of our ability."

"I can't remember when I realized that I was merely mortal and no longer immortal, but I do know that it was after I turned 30."

"It's not so much where you have been that matters, but rather where you are going. That is why it is so important to have a plan."

"Excellence, like anything else worthwhile, never comes easily. It requires our best efforts, diligence, as well as a degree of endurance."

"There is nothing greater in this world than our personal honor and integrity."

"I hate labels because they are often nothing more than a manifestation of someone being un-righteously judgmental. I hate it when someone is labeled and forever pigeon-holed…. especially a child."

"First impressions are everything!"

"Aim for the center of the bull's eye, and you will likely hit the target."

"Character really is the sum total of what you believe, how you act, and how you react to circumstances beyond your control."

"There is no such thing as over preparation."

"Whether it is closing for the appointment or the sale, 'overlearning' your skills instills confidence and a higher level of expectations."

"Be observant. It is amazing what you will notice and learn."

"Praise in Public correct in private. Nobody wants to be made into a spectacle."

Observations

"Is there anything more powerful and inviting than the sunrise over the water?"

"If something sounds too good to be true, it usually is, so don't be fooled."

"We are like rocks in a running stream. We can either allow the friction of the water to polish us up or to wear us down."

"Other people can put obstacles in your way, but only you can decide when you are going to stop pursuing that path."

"If you want to learn to swim you have to get into the pool. Somebody else can't learn for you."

"Is there anything sweeter than a slice of ice-cold watermelon on a sweltering summer day?"

"Trust is the foundation of every relationship that we enjoy. We must be true to ourselves, to our family, our faith, and to those we lead."

"One kind word is often better and easier remembered than a thousand unkind ones. Never same something in anger that you are going to regret later. You can't un-ring the bell."

"Be discreet in your indiscretions."

"You can't give a man pride, but you can rob him of it."

"Truth may be stranger than fiction, but it is easier to remember too. Telling the truth requires less memory."

"The truth may hurt, but a lie is agony."

"We are all born with the same limitations of time, physical abilities, and natural intelligence. It is us to us to take these ordinary attributes and make them into some extraordinary."

"As it has been said, no man is an island. We are a compilation of all the people and elements that have influenced us throughout our lives. The challenge is to resist the negative influences and to firmly embrace the positive."

"It's not enough to be smart – one must know *when* to be smart."

"Never settle for the path of least resistance.
It usually only leads downward."

"Is it for us to judge whether the sunrise or
the sunset is of greater beauty?"

"From time to time you may have to stretch the truth in the form of a white lie in order to spare someone's feelings or for some other noble reason. Keep in mind however, if you lie to yourself, you will always lose."

"Easy jobs don't pay much. If you want to make a good living and provide a higher lifestyle for your family, you have to either obtain education that sets you apart like your friendly neighborhood brain surgeon or be willing to do something nobody else wants to do such as being a garbage collector or the guy who transports porta potties."

"Is there anything as forlorn as an empty gum ball machine?"

"Why does it take so long for people to board a plane? Why can't they only bring proper sized luggage on board? Why can't they stow it in accordance with written and oral directions? Why does the guy who insists on stowing BOTH pieces of his luggage in the overhead bin, thus keeping his leg room completely free, always sit in front of me where I am aware of the situation?"

"Reading is one of Life's purest delights. Whether it is for entertainment, education, or edification, what a wonderful gift it is to be able to wander off between the covers of a book and simply read. For me, the joy of holding a favorite book will never be replaced by the iPhone, iPad, or computer monitor."

"Each one of the books that I have had a hand in creating is like an addition to my family. The day the first copy arrives is nearly on par with the arrival of each of our children. Naming them was easier though."

"A good book is like a friend... one to be savored and enjoyed."

"I used to laugh when Jay Leno interviewed people on the street and they did not know who the current Vice President was, or they did not recognize something that was being carried as front page news. Now, I am gravely concerned that we are raising a generation of historically illiterate people. My own kids turned their noses up at sites such as Jamestown, Williamsburg, Monticello, Mount Vernon. It was not until we were empty nesters that we were truly able to enjoy walking where the likes of Jefferson, Washington, and Lee had trod."

"I was thrilled the other day when two of my grandchildren *wanted* to see pictures from our trip to Paris, France. They were captivated by the Eiffel Tower, amazed that we had stood on it, much less had a private black-tie affair on it, equally awed by all the gold present in the pictures of our tour of Versailles, as well as the other sights of Paris. Imagine my surprise when they could not grasp that many of the pictures were of sites three hundred years old – older than anything in the United States."

"No matter how old I am, I am still amazed at Man's inhumanity to one another as the headlines are filled with reports of hate crimes and murder committed in various houses of worship."

"Video games that de-sensitize players to extreme violence and killing will certainly blur the line between fantasy and reality and contribute to the ever growing scourge that is impacting our country."

"I can remember Neil Armstrong walking on the moon; the stain of Vietnam and the moratorium; the deaths of John F. Kennedy, Martin Luther King Jr, and Robert F. Kennedy; the horror of 9-11 and the terror of the twin towers falling; because this is NOT history to me but rather our life. It is history to our children and grandchildren. The challenge is to remember that history does not start out as history but as life... we are part of it as it unfolds around us."

"Pride is a foolish man's luxury, usually ill-afforded."

"It is important that we are always battling against complacency in all aspects of our lives. Just as our bodies can develop both positive and negative muscle memory, we must avoid allowing our brains and spiritual pursuits from going on autopilot thus halting our progression."

"You are a direct reflection of the people with whom you spend time. Choose them carefully."

"Major Brent Taylor. A fifteen year veteran of the Utah National Guard returned two months early from his FOURTH deployment overseas, on our November 2018 election day… in a flag-draped coffin. Murdered by someone purportedly 'on our side' we add his name to the list of senseless sacrifice. Rather than resuming his post as Mayor of North Ogden, UT (from which he was on a leave of absence) and returning to his wife and seven children, he is gone forever. His last message to his family even referenced the 'near sacred rite' that voting in free elections should be considered.

As usual, I shed tears watching the casket coming off the cargo plane at Dover Air Force Base. I have a lump in my throat as I recall the video and must seriously wonder if I will ever be able to watch such events and not shed these tears of gratitude at the ultimate sacrifice being paid."

"Trust in yourself. That little voice that speaks to you will usually never let you down."

"School plays and performances ... it's exponential as the amount of audience time multiplies with the growing number of grandchildren."

"There really is something timeless about Christmas music as memories can come flooding back and we are transported back to what appears to be simpler times."

"The annual holiday letter: fact or fiction? Like an acne cream we remove the blemishes and leave only the smooth skin as we want to be viewed."

"It's one thing to track your 'firsts' in a new job or church calling; but what would it be like to know that this is probably your last Christmas with your family because of a life-threatening illness? How stoic would you be with this knowledge at hand?"

"It always pays to dress one level above the job for which you are applying, showing respect for the interviewer and the process. But remember, as the hiring authority that better dressed does not necessarily mean better qualified. Don't fall into the trap of judging a book by its cover."

"The louder you yell, the less they will hear you."

Opportunity

"I was four years old when the world lived on the brink of nuclear annihilation in October 1962. Books and movie treatments have been created that attempt to capture the drama and brinksmanship as the world collectively held its breath as the United States and the USSR literally and figuratively negotiated the waters around Cuba and the nuclear missiles that had been placed there for no other reason than to intimidate the United States. That snippet of time has been immortalized as *The Cuban Missile Crisis* and as *Thirteen Days.* I studied it in grammar school and high school as part of my history class, later as an Army officer in various seminars dealing in leadership, and finally on my own as a student of the world around me. While there were many military, political, and leadership lessons to be gleaned, the single largest takeaway for me to internalize as a student of life is that summarized by President John F. Kennedy who noted that *'when written in Chinese, the word 'crisis' is composed of two characters. One represents danger, and the other represents opportunity.'* I think we all must remember those characterizations as we face crises in our own lives. When we change our approach to obstacles and recognize them as opportunities, they are not nearly as insurmountable and overwhelming."

"Become a good listener. Sometimes when Opportunity knocks, it is hard to discern with all the white noise that surrounds us."

"My grandfather lived his life as a series of 'couldas, wouldas, shouldas.' The lesson that I took away from watching him is that when Opportunity comes knocking, you have to be willing to answer the door."

"Sadly, most of us are afraid of Opportunity because when we encounter it, it looks like more time and effort than we are willing to invest. Don't be afraid to sacrifice the short term for the long term if the evidence pointing to long term success is genuinely apparent."

"Nothing is more painful or regretted, than a missed opportunity. Don't allow your life to become a series of coulda, shoulda, woulda experiences. Go for it!"

"Life holds no problems, only challenges and opportunities in which to grow."

"With great opportunity and success comes an accompanying expectation for us to give back."

"Serving others is not a burden but rather a wonderful opportunity where we not only better them but also ourselves."

"Albert Einstein is probably best remembered for his Theory of Relativity. I prefer his Three Rules of Work:

1. Out of clutter find simplicity...
2. From discord find harmony…
3. In difficulty, find opportunity."

"Don't be afraid of opportunity…it may very well change your life in a way that you have never previously imagined."

"If you have the opportunity to change careers, just get on with it. After I changed careers, I met many of my former peers who praised my courage and 'gumption for going for it.' Just because you are secure or 'comfortable' don't hesitate to make the change if you determine that 'happy' is not a word that you are using to describe yourself."

"When considering new opportunities, make sure that you also consider the consequences and not just the ancillary rewards."

"What may appear to be a certain opportunity may actually turn out to be a gateway to yet a completely different opportunity."

"Every day is another opportunity for us to improve ourselves, our lives, as well as that of those around us. Don't squander these opportunities, for we are all provided only a finite number of them."

"Like the acres of diamonds that we often overlook in our own backyard, it is the same with opportunities. Sometimes these opportunities are there in plain sight, but we choose not to see them."

"Opportunities come in different shapes and sizes and often require us to discern between good, better and best by weighing rewards and consequences against our priorities."

Parenting & Family

"This is an adventure fraught with danger
and a wild range of emotions."

"As parents, we agreed that it was not our job to build a highway network for our children, replete with rest stops, but rather to provide them with a road atlas that they could use as a reference as they navigate from point to point in their adult lives. Fortunately, there is now GPS for them to fall back on as well."

"Whether it is at work or at home, if you have to mete out discipline or correction remember to do it in the form of a love sandwich. Let them know you love them, correct them, and slap another slice of love to complete the sandwich."

"My heart absolutely sings when I see one of my children brimming with confidence before embracing a challenge that could define their future."
August 2018

"The mark of maturity is when your child can discern between needs and wants. It usually happens when they start paying for their own stuff."

"While it is important to raise up your children in righteousness, it is equally important to raise them to be self-reliant."

"I was sitting in an audience of three thousand other leaders listening to leadership-guru John Maxwell when he shared a great learning from his own life: 'grandchildren are our reward for not killing our own children.' He may very well be right. It is what makes being parents the second time around so grand an experience… and no diapers either."

"Teach your children well, and leave no greater legacy than an honest and true heart."

"My role as a parent has not been to make all the right choices for my children but to teach them how to reason and to make proper choices for themselves."

"As parents, it is our responsibility to demand the best effort possible from our children and ourselves, and then to be satisfied with these results."

"You never stop worrying; you never stop trying; because the problems and challenges will always be there.... only bigger and more expensive."

"I can still remember quite vividly when at age 10, I learned the basic law that for every action there is a reaction. I have since referred to it as "T-H-I-N-K." Nobody taught it to me, I merely discovered it as if by accident. I remember that I was playing catch by myself by throwing a rubber ball against the house. At times I was also practicing my pitching, so I was really bringing the heat. Suddenly it occurred to me that if I threw the ball either too hard or without proper control that I could break a window or worse, the patio sliding glass door. I had visions of being an indentured servant for years and years if that were to occur. I remember standing there, ball in hand, contemplating all the various ways that I could bring down ruin upon myself. Thereafter, I was always very careful about throwing things or doing anything that I myself would consider 'stupid.' Surprisingly, I have to remind myself of this lesson repeatedly...."

"As parents, our job is to make our homes a sanctuary of unconditional safety, peace, acceptance and spirituality."

"We encouraged our children when they were young to make certain decisions only once, e.g. not drinking alcohol, smoking cigarettes, or messing around with drugs of any kind. Once these decisions were made, they were seemingly immune to peer pressure or temptation that may come along."

"As parents we all feel a desire, or even a duty, to shield our children from the vulgarity and ugliness that the world has to offer. Today, one of our largest challenges is to protect our children from the evils of images that come into our home via television and the Internet. We attempt to shield our children from these images that can first desensitize and then to forever stain their souls. Gratefully, none of us must physically shield our children from the ravages of an existence where continued life, or the finality of death, can be decided and assigned by the mere pointing of a finger or the nod of a head." Excerpt from *The Gazebo*

"Doctors and attorneys get to practice their craft. Why don't we get the same luxury as parents?"

"Rules are good things to have, but I would probably have been wiser to remember that we were dealing with people."

"Changing times require flexibility even when dealing with children and the establishment of, or adherence to rules."

"Even the best of parents with the purest and most idealistic intentions of providing a better life for their children can set them up for failure by confusing better with easier."

"We recently shared the dinner table with friends who are much older than ourselves and shared the concerns of our heart as they pertained to our children and grandchildren. Much to our amazement they too harbored the same concerns. It was at that moment that we saw the exhaustion in their eyes and faces and realized that they have been giving their all for the benefit of their family and knew that this was another example of enduring to the end."

"It seems like only yesterday that we were racing to the hospital with some degree of biannual frequency as each of our children decided to make their loud and raucous entrance into the world. I'll never forget the anticipation that accompanied the nine months of waiting, wondering, dreaming, hoping, and praying. With nearly thirty years intervening since the last experience, it is now easy to overlook, and nearly forget, the sudden mood swings, the uncontrollable cravings at all hours of the night which in turn led to the extra weight around the middle, the sore back, as well as the sleepless nights. Then there were all the symptoms that my wife experienced as well during the pregnancies. But what can't be forgotten are those feelings of pure anticipation and joy with which we greeted each of the actual delivery experiences. Of course it was easier for me than it was for their mom, because all I had to do was to stay out of the way, voice encouragement to the mother-to-be generally, and coaching her to breathe without hyperventilating specifically, and when the time was right, to literally cut the umbilical cord, and amuse the doctor while I wrestled with those darned *right-handed* scissors. Nonetheless, never under estimate the amount of stress that the father feels during this incredible miracle-like time.

The stress is different, obviously far less physical, but is there, nonetheless. Thoughts of our own shortcomings and inadequacies, our ability to nurture another child, and to produce another contributing member of society are just a sliver of the myriad of thoughts that go through our mind as we first lay eyes on that new bundle of joy. Will he or she be a scholar? Or manifest the catlike reflexes and prowess of a great athlete? How many great accomplishments will find their roots in the actions of this newborn?

We are left to wonder, sometimes in complete awe, at what we can best describe as our seeds; and wonder how many apples this seed will in turn bear over the next series of generations. What great and marvelous acts will come from this small child or their progeny?"

- excerpt from *Mom and Dad Leadership*

"In terms of discipline and the rearing of our children, Sebastian the Crab may have said it best in *Little Mermaid* when he advised the King, 'give them an inch, and they swim all over you.' The key is to be fair, firm, and resolute."

"The next time you are doing a crossword puzzle or watching *Jeopardy*! and the question comes up for a three letter word or phrase that means cash dispenser... the correct answer is A-T-M... and not D-A-D... though it may very often feel like it should be the latter."

"Children may not always listen to us, but they will quickly imitate us...particularly if the example we set is not one of which we should be proud."

"Only love can be divided repeatedly, and never have its effects diminished."

"I love the idea of being a great-grandparent (especially at such a young age), and feel pretty good about taking a great-grandmother out to dinner on date night, but who wants a grandfather for their own kid?"

"To create memories for your children to enjoy in the future you have to be present with them today."

"Graveyards are full of indispensable people who gave their employers a 24/7 effort. I was in danger of being one of those people until it was pointed out to me that while my work is important it is not more important than the work I was completing within the wall of my home, as the patriarch of my family."

"It never ceases to amaze me how our children can tease us for maintaining certain family traditions, and yet, if we deviate from them, they criticize us for abandoning them. Maybe that is another tradition in itself!"

"We know that human nature dictates that every person wants to be part of something bigger than themselves. The ultimate organization is the eternal family. Isn't it amazing how easily we can take ours for granted?"

"It is fun for me to watch my own children forming traditions for their own families, as they blend with those of their spouse and their family. This exercise is an extension of our legacy."

"Family should not be a priority. It should be THE priority."

"The greatest gift that we can receive from God is our family. Isn't it a shame that we so often take it for granted until it is irretrievably or prematurely taken from us?"

RELATIONSHIPS

"The first ten years of marriage is hard. It is not so much a matter of dealing with the commonalities that attracted you to one another, but rather getting used to those things that distinguish one from the other."

"Trust is the foundation of every relationship that we enjoy. We must be true to ourselves, to our family, our faith, and to those we lead."

"The key to a long and happy life is to fall in love many times in the course of your life.... with the same person."

"If you are thinking in terms of filling human needs, remember that the most important emotional need is to be appreciated."

"We are all interdependent. There is no such thing as being off the grid. Because we need one another, we need to be accessible and approachable. A smile indicates that we are ready to receive."

"Life really is about the relationships we experience during the journey of life. Some relationships will leave profound and indelible imprints on our life, while others may resemble chance encounters. Some will be enjoyable, others less so. The key is to take something away from each of these relationships and in the years to come, pay proper attribution for the lessons we learned."

"If you can develop the ability to find the good in people, and in given situations, you will be the benefactor of strong and rewarding relationships."

"We will be judged on the manner in which we maintained relationships in our lives."

"The mobility of our society has changed its very fiber. We no longer put down roots, with the expectation of remaining in the same community for a lifetime, much less live in one home for a lifetime, or in a multi-generational setting. It is now common for friendships, business relationships, and family relationships to be intercontinental. We must guard against complacency in all of our relationships, and build them up, layer upon layer, so that they remain eternal in their nature."

"Relationships get better and stronger when both parties remember the principle of forgiveness."

"Your relationships will be better when you realize that people are not perfect, and that it is about accepting one another's foibles."

"It is true love when we care more about the other person's happiness than our own."

To be successful, every relationship has to be based on Trust."

"The foundational element of a relationship has to be respect. You cannot maintain a façade of a relationship if you do not honestly respect the other person and they both *know* and *reciprocate* this respect."

"Relationships have to be bilateral in nature. A unilateral or one-sided relationship is always doomed to failure. One person always giving and the other person always taking is a recipe for disaster."

"A solid relationship continues to grow, and even in professional settings, can foster friendship."

"A good relationship requires real effort and is always better when both parties are focused on understanding the other person rather than being understood themselves."

"Everybody wants to be a somebody. You have the ability to make them feel like a somebody by simply recognizing what they do and attaching significance to it."

"Despite song lyrics and great odes penned by the masters, no man is an island. Everybody needs somebody and to be needed by somebody."

"The greatest gift that we can give another person is the ability to believe in themselves and their capabilities."

"When you think highly of someone, and they know it, you are then empowered to say just about anything you want as a coach or a mentor."

"People are not going to respond to you as a leader until they know and understand you as a person. The utilization of raw leadership authority is no different than the 'because I said so,' that so many of us endured growing up as children."

"The ultimate way to demonstrate respect for another person is to be present and fully engaged in listening when they are speaking."

"Being a good listener will allow you to connect with more people in less time than if you try to talk your way into relationships."

"Over the years I have appreciated many relationships in which I was the student and the other person was the teacher. What made these relationships so special is that I knew that these people were truly and honestly invested in my success, and the only thing I needed to do to show my gratitude was to listen and to subsequently apply the lessons that they were attempting to impart to me."

"The greatest way to show appreciation for another person is to listen to them when they are attempting to convey a thought, an emotion, or more importantly a need of their own."

"One of my pet peeves are people who profess to being great listeners and subsequently don't allow me to string two sentences together without an interruption."

"Effective listening is more than just hearing the words. It is about parsing them for meaning and truly understanding what the other person is attempting to communicate to you. This is especially important in our personal relationships."

"The best way to enhance and preserve relationships of all kinds is to avoid the poison associated with being judgmental."

Rites of Passage

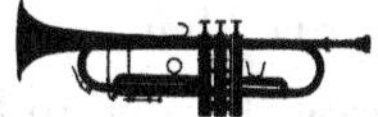

Rites of Passage

In the course of my tenure as a Bishop in the Church of Jesus Christ of Latter Day Saints, I had the privilege of officiating at about a dozen marriage ceremonies, an equal number of ring ceremonies for marriages solemnized in the Temple, an occasional civil ceremony, as well as several funerals for congregants, friends, or my own family members. For each of the marriages, I wrote a separate ceremony and printed a copy of it on parchment paper to be shared with the happy couple in their Book of Remembrance. These ceremonies were by far the most fun thing I did, especially when I arrived at the wedding site with the groom and best man via speedboat on the Chickahominy River. The following are representative of what I consider to be some of my most important, life-altering writing efforts.

RING CEREMONY

We welcome all of you here today.

You may be aware that the temple is a place that we do proxy work for the dead that includes baptism, endowment, and sealing. But more importantly, it is also a place for the living.

Young people like Michael and Mary are encouraged to marry in the Temple. For us here in Virginia, that means battling our way up I-95 to the Washington D.C. Temple located in Kensington, MD. But Mike and Mary said the heck with that traffic and were sealed last weekend in the Las Vegas Temple. This is one time where what happens in Vegas decidedly does not stay in Vegas.

While in the Temple Michael and Mary took part in a ceremony called a Sealing, which was officiated over by a priesthood holder authorized to perform this ordinance. The intent of this ceremony was to seal them as husband and wife not only for life in this world but for the eternities.

The purpose of a temple marriage, referred to in the scriptures as the new and everlasting covenant of marriage (D&C 131:2), is to seal a husband and wife for time and eternity, depending on their faithfulness. Through this ordinance, a couple's children may also be part of their eternal family. Only a marriage that has been sealed in the Temple and confirmed by the Holy Spirit of Promise can be eternal (D&C 132:7).

The sealing ceremony is very precise as it is a covenant not only between Michael and Mary, but rather between them and the Lord. For if they truly have a celestial marriage, the partnership will be comprised of not only these two fine young people but also the Lord.

Because of this precision, no rings or traditional vows are exchanged. At this time, Michael and Mary wish to exchange rings with one another as outward symbols of their love for one another, and to do so in the presence of all of you.

The ring has long been the symbol for the sealing of important contracts. In the early history of Man, the King wore a ring upon which was pressed the seal of the Kingdom. With this ring he sealed the treaties of the land. But in more recent generations the ring has been used to seal the marriage contract.

You may now exchange rings. [Exchange Rings].

May this beautiful token and pledge symbolize the purity and never ending love you have for your chosen companion in life.

Mike and Mary, may you always be as happy as you are today, with your love growing stronger with each passing day as you place one another's needs ahead of your own. Honor all the covenants that you made in the temple and the blessings of Heaven will be yours.

May God bless your union with joy in your posterity and a long life of happiness together, and may He enable you to keep these sacred covenants that you have entered into. These blessings I invoke upon you in the name of the Lord Jesus Christ, amen.

CIVIL WEDDING CEREMONY

"Please take each other by the right hand."

"Groom's full name and Bride's full name, you have taken one another by the right hand in token of the covenants you will now enter into in the presence of God and these witnesses." the couple may choose or nominate these witnesses.]

"Groom's full name, do you take Bride's full name, as your lawfully wedded wife, and do you of your own free will and choice covenant as her companion and lawfully wedded husband that you will cleave unto her and none else; that you will observe all the laws, covenants, and obligations pertaining to the holy state of matrimony; and that you will love, honor, and cherish her as long as you both shall live?" [He answers "Yes" or "I do."]

"Bride's full name, do you take Groom's full name, as your lawfully wedded husband, and do you of your own free will and choice covenant as his companion and lawfully wedded wife that you will cleave unto him and none else; that you will observe all the laws, covenants, and obligations pertaining to the holy state of matrimony; and that you will love, honor, and cherish him as long as you both shall live?" [She answers "Yes" or "I do."]

"By virtue of the legal authority vested in me as an elder of The Church of Jesus Christ of Latter-day Saints, I pronounce you, Groom's full name and Bride's full name, husband and wife, legally and lawfully wedded for the period of your mortal lives."

"May God bless your union with joy in your posterity and a long life of happiness together, and may He enable you to keep sacred the covenants you have made. These blessings I invoke upon you in the name of the Lord Jesus Christ, amen."

"You may kiss each other as husband and wife."

WEDDING CEREMONY

ONE OF THE GREATEST HUMAN DESIRES IS TO LOVE AND TO BE LOVED. FOR THIS REASON, WE HAVE GATHERED HERE IN THE PRESENCE OF GOD AND THIS COMPANY OF LOVED ONES, AS FAMILY AND FRIENDS OF JOHN AND MARY, TO WITNESS THEIR LOVE MADE MANIFEST IN THIS UNION TODAY; A MAN AND WOMAN JOINING THEIR LIVES

TO BECOME HUSBAND AND WIFE. WE APPRECIATE YOUR BEING HERE TO CELEBRATE THIS SPECIAL OCCASION.

FROM THE BEGINNING OF CREATION, GOD MADE THEM MALE AND FEMALE. AND GOD SAID, "IT IS NOT GOOD FOR MAN TO BE ALONE. I WILL MAKE A HELPMEET FOR HIM." AND GOD CAUSED A SLEEP TO FALL UPON ADAM AND HE SLEPT, AND HE TOOK ONE OF HIS RIBS AND CLOSED UP THE FLESH THEREOF. AND FROM THE RIB THE LORD GOD HAD TAKEN

FROM THE MAN MADE HE A WOMAN AND SHE SHALL BE CALLED WOMAN BECAUSE SHE WAS TAKEN OUT OF MAN.

WHEN GOD CREATED WOMAN FROM THE RIB OF MAN, SHE WAS NOT MADE OUT OF HIS HEAD TO RULE OVER HIM, NOR OUT OF HIS FEET TO BE TRAMPLED UPON BY HIM, BUT OUT OF HIS SIDE TO BE HIS EQUAL AND TO WALK BESIDE HIM, UNDER HIS ARM TO BE PROTECTED, AND NEAR HIS HEART TO BE LOVED.

MARRIAGE IS PERHAPS THE MOST VITAL OF ALL THE DECISIONS WE MAKE. IT AFFECTS NOT ONLY OUR LIVES, BUT THE LIVES OF EXISTING FAMILY, AND MORE IMPORTANTLY THE CHILDREN THAT OUR HEAVENLY FATHER WILL ENTRUST TO US, AS WELL AS THEIR POSTERITY.

A SUCCESSFUL MARRIAGE, A HAPPY MARRIAGE DOES NOT COME BY WISHFUL THINKING OR FROM PURE HOPE, BUT WITH HARD AND DILIGENT WORK FROM BOTH PARTNERS. IT IS NOT A 50-50 PARTNERSHIP AS YOU MAY HAVE HEARD, BUT ONE IN WHICH BOTH PARTNERS EXPEND 110% EFFORT, SOMETIMES ONE CARRYING THE OTHER, AND AT OTHER TIMES, THE ROLES REVERSED.

HAPPINESS IS A STATE OF MIND AND COMES FROM WITHIN. HAPPINESS DOES NOT MEAN THERE WILL BE NO PROBLEMS; IT DOES NOT MEAN THAT WHEN THINGS OCCASIONALLY GET ROUGH THAT YOU CUT AND RUN. WHAT IT DOES MEAN IS THAT THE TWO OF YOU WILL BE ABLE TO FACE THESE TRIALS AND TRIBULATIONS TOGETHER, AND THROUGH YOUR UNITED EFFORTS BE ABLE TO OVERCOME THEM.

THERE ARE SOME RULES WHICH WILL HELP YOU ACHIEVE THIS HAPPINESS OF WHICH WE SPEAK.

FIRST, REMEMBER THAT IN ORDER TO BE EFFECTIVE, YOUR UNION HAS THREE MEMBERS: JOHN, MARY, AND THE LORD. NEVER IGNORE ANY MEMBER OF THIS TRILOGY AS YOU CONTEMPLATE DECISIONS THAT NEED TO BE MADE.

SECOND, MAKE YOUR HOME A CHRIST-CENTERED HOME. STARTING TODAY, MAKE DAILY PRAYER A HABIT IN YOUR HOME. MAKE READING THE SCRIPTURES A PRIORITY. PUT THE LORD FIRST IN ALL THINGS YOU PLAN AND DO.

THIRD, BE SELFLESS. PLACE THE TEMPORAL, PHYSICAL, SPIRITUAL, AND EMOTIONAL NEEDS OF YOUR COMPANION AHEAD OF YOUR OWN. JUST AS THERE IS NO 'I' IN THE WORD TEAM, YOU MUST ALSO FORGET PHRASES SUCH AS 'I WANT', AND 'I NEED', AND INSTEAD REPLACE THEM WITH 'OUR', 'US' AND 'WE'.

FOURTH, REMEMBER THE VERY THINGS THAT MADE YOU FALL IN LOVE WITH ONE ANOTHER AND NEVER STOP DOING THEM FOR ONE ANOTHER. JOHN, IF IT WAS OPENING DOORS FOR HER, KEEP ON DOING THAT. IF IT WAS BAKING COOKIES FOR HIM, FATTEN HIM UP!

FIFTH, NEVER GROW TOO OLD FOR DATE NIGHT, OR HOLDING HANDS.

SIXTH, REMEMBER THAT LIFE CAN CHANGE IN THE BLINK OF AN EYE. SAY 'I LOVE YOU' AT LEAST ONCE A DAY.

SEVENTH, NEVER TAKE ONE ANOTHER FOR GRANTED. TODAY IS NOT AN ENDING, BUT RATHER A BEGINNING OF THE JOURNEY INTO ETERNITY.

LEARN TO FORGIVE AND TO FORGET. THAT IS THE PATTERN THAT THE LORD HAS ESTABLISHED AND WHICH YOU MUST FOLLOW AS WELL IF YOU WANT TO ACHIEVE TOTAL HAPPINESS.

YOU DON'T NEED TO HAVE THE LAST WORD OR WORDS, UNLESS THEY ARE 'YES, DEAR.' TO THIS END, NEVER GO TO BED ANGRY WITH ONE ANOTHER. TALK PROBLEMS THROUGH WITHOUT BEING DEMEANING OR DISRESPECTFUL.

DO THINGS FOR ONE ANOTHER WITH A GLAD HEART AND NOT IN AN ATTITUDE OF DUTY OR SACRIFICE. REMEMBER TOO, THAT THERE IS GREAT JOY IN GIVING OF OUR HEART.

BE A RIGHTEOUS EXAMPLE TO YOUR CHILDREN. JOHN, THE GREATEST GIFT THAT A FATHER CAN GIVE TO HIS CHILDREN IS TO LOVE THEIR MOTHER. BE DEMONSTRATIVE IN YOUR AFFECTIONS. LET YOUR CHILDREN SEE THE LOVE YOU FEEL FOR ONE ANOTHER MANIFESTED OFTEN. IT IS IN THESE MOMENTS THAT YOU ARE PLANTING SEEDS OF AN ETERNAL NATURE FOR YOUR POSTERITY.

REMEMBER TOO, THAT THE MOST IMPORTANT WORK THAT YOU WILL DO IN THIS LIFE WILL BE WITHIN THE FOUR WALLS OF YOUR HOME. NO DEGREE OF SUCCESS OUTSIDE OF THE HOME WILL EVER COMPENSATE FOR FAILURE WITHIN THE HOME.

MARY, IT IS NOT EXPECTING JOHN TO WEAR A HALO, OR JOHN, FOR MARY TO HAVE WINGS LIKE AN ANGEL. IT IS NOT LOOKING FOR PERFECTION IN EACH OTHER; IT IS BEING FLEXIBLE, PATIENT, UNDERSTANDING, AND HAVING A SENSE OF HUMOR.

IT IS ABOUT BEING TOLERANT AND FORGIVING. IT IS HELPING ONE ANOTHER TO GROW. IT IS NOT ABOUT MARRYING THE RIGHT PARTNER BUT BEING THE RIGHT PARTNER. OUR THOUGHTS BECOME OUR ACTIONS.

FROM THIS DAY FORWARD, WORK TOWARDS THE DAY THAT YOU MAY ATTEND THE TEMPLE AND ENTER THE HOUSE OF THE LORD WITH THE INTENT OF HAVING YOUR MARRIAGE SEALED FOR ALL TIME AND ETERNITY; SO THAT YOUR CHILDREN CAN BE BORN IN THE COVENANT, AND THAT YOU CAN BE A TRULY ETERNAL COUPLE AND FAMILY.

THE SCRIPTURES ARE REPLETE WITH SUGGESTIONS, AND LET ME PARAPHRASE A FEW OF THEM FOR YOU:

MARY, LET THY SOUL DELIGHT IN YOUR HUSBAND; SUBMIT YOURSELF UNTO JOHN AS UNTO THE LORD, FOR THE HUSBAND IS THE HEAD OF THE WIFE, EVEN AS CHRIST IS THE HEAD OF THE CHURCH.

JOHN, LOVE YOUR WIFE MARY WITH ALL THY HEART AND CLEAVE UNTO HER EVEN AS YOURSELF. GIVE HONOR

UNTO HER. REMEMBER, THAT IF THE HUSBAND IS THE HEAD, THEN THE WIFE IS THE NECK FROM WHICH THE HEAD RECEIVES DIRECTION.

IF YOU WILL DO THESE THINGS YOU WILL HAVE A HAPPY MARRIAGE.

PLEASE TAKE EACH OTHER BY THE RIGHT HAND.

JOHN QUINCY ADAMS AND MARY TYLER MOORE, YOU HAVE TAKEN ONE ANOTHER BY THE RIGHT HAND IN TOKEN OF THE COVENANTS YOU WILL NOW ENTER INTO IN THE PRESENCE OF GOD AND THESE WITNESSES.

JOHN QUINCY ADAMS DO YOU TAKE MARY TYLER MOORE AS YOUR LAWFULLY WEDDED WIFE, AND DO YOU OF YOUR OWN FREE WILL AND CHOICE COVENANT AS HER COMPANION AND LAWFULLY WEDDED HUSBAND THAT YOU WILL CLEAVE UNTO HER AND NONE ELSE? THAT YOU WILL OBSERVE ALL THE LAWS, COVENANTS, AND OBLIGATIONS PERTAINING TO THE HOLY STATE OF MATRIMONY, AND THAT YOU WILL LOVE, HONOR, AND CHERISH HER AS LONG AS YOU BOTH SHALL LIVE?

[RESPONSE] – "YES."

MARY TYLER MOORE DO YOU TAKE JOHN QUINCY ADAMS AS YOUR LAWFULLY WEDDED HUSBAND, AND DO YOU OF YOUR OWN FREE WILL AND CHOICE COVENANT AS HIS COMPANION AND LAWFULLY WEDDED WIFE THAT YOU WILL CLEAVE UNTO HIM AND NONE ELSE? THAT YOU WILL OBSERVE ALL THE LAWS, COVENANTS, AND OBLIGATIONS PERTAINING TO THE HOLY STATE OF MATRIMONY, AND THAT YOU WILL LOVE, HONOR, AND CHERISH HIM AS LONG AS YOU BOTH SHALL LIVE?

[RESPONSE] – “YES.”

<u>*ASK FOR THE RING(S)*</u>
THE RING HAS LONG BEEN THE SYMBOL FOR THE SEALING OF IMPORTANT CONTRACTS. IN THE EARLIER HISTORY OF MAN, THE KING WORE A RING UPON WHICH WAS PRESSED THE SEAL OF THE KINGDOM. WITH THIS RING HE SEALED THE TREATIES OF THE LAND. BUT IN MORE RECENT GENERATIONS THE RING HAS BEEN USED TO SEAL THE MARRIAGE CONTRACT.

THE RING TEACHES US MANY LESSONS. THE PURITY OF ITS METAL REMINDS US OF THE PURITY OF YOUR LOVE FOR EACH OTHER. THE ENDLESS CIRCLE REMINDS US OF THE ETERNAL NATURE OF YOUR LOVE. THE WEDDING RING IS AN OUTWARD AND VISIBLE SIGN OF AN INWARD AND SPIRITUAL BOND WHICH UNITES TWO LOYAL HEARTS AS ONE.

MAY THIS BEAUTIFUL TOKEN AND PLEDGE SYMBOLIZE THE PURITY AND NEVER ENDING LOVE YOU HAVE FOR YOUR CHOSEN COMPANION IN THIS LIFE.

<u>*REPEAT AFTER ME:*</u>
JOHN: “MARY, THIS RING I GIVE THEE IN TOKEN AND PLEDGE, OF OUR CONSTANT FAITH AND ABIDING LOVE.”

MARY: “JOHN, THIS RING I GIVE THEE IN TOKEN AND PLEDGE, OF OUR CONSTANT FAITH AND ABIDING LOVE.”

BY VIRTUE OF THE LEGAL AUTHORITY VESTED IN ME BY THE COMMONWEALTH OF VIRGINIA AS AN ELDER OF THE CHURCH OF JESUS CHRIST OF LATTER DAY SAINTS, I PRONOUCE YOU JOHN QUINCY ADAMS AND MARY TYLER

MOORE, HUSBAND AND WIFE, LEGALLY AND LAWFULLY WEDDED FOR THE PERIOD OF YOUR MORTAL LIVES.

MAY THE JOY OF THIS DAY NEVER GROW DIM; MAY ITS MEMORIES BECOME SWEETER AND TENDER WITH EACH PASSING ANNIVERSARY.

MAY GOD BLESS YOUR UNION WITH JOY IN ONE ANOTHER AND IN YOUR POSTERITY, AND A LONG AND FRUITFUL LIFE FULL OF HAPPINESS TOGETHER, AND MAY HE ENABLE YOU TO KEEP SACRED THE COVENANTS YOU HAVE MADE HERE TODAY. THESE BLESSINGS I INVOKE UPON YOU IN THE SACRED NAME OF OUR LORD AND SAVIOR, EVEN JESUS CHRIST, AMEN.

YOU MAY NOW KISS EACH OTHER AS HUSBAND AND WIFE.

LADIES AND GENTLEMEN, I PRESENT MR. AND MRS. JOHN QUINCY ADAMS

For as wonderful as officiating at a wedding is, there are other rites of passage. When we leave our probationary mortal state, and transition to the next state, there is often a great deal of sadness. Fortunately, as members of the Church of Jesus Christ of Latter Day Saints we believe in the eternal nature of families and that when sealed as a couple and family, that we will be reunited with our loved ones again.

I was asked to officiate at the funeral for the brother of a member of my congregation. He was not a member of our church, but his sister felt that this would be an opportune moment to introduce the concept of eternal families to her grieving parents, other members of her family, as well as friends who had gathered to remember her brother. I later used this very talk as part of my novel *The Advocate.*

"On behalf of the Pritchard family, I would like to welcome and thank all of you who have come to pay your respects to Annabelle and show support for her parents, Bill and Evie, as well as her sister Crystal, brothers Carter and Andrew, and other family members.

Many of you are here today with your hearts full of grief as you contemplate how much Annabelle will be missed, how unfair it seems that she should have had to suffer with the cancer that ravaged and withered her body, especially after the pain and anguish that Annabelle suffered when the life of her husband John and daughters Emily and Caitlin were so abruptly, and tragically, cut short just a few short years ago at the hands of a drunk driver.

Many of you are here with a great number of questions as you contemplate why such a senseless tragedy was allowed to occur; where Annabelle and John and their daughters are now; where you will go when it is your time to depart the Earth; whether there really is a Heaven; or whether any of us will ever see Annabelle and her family again. I want to share with you some of the beliefs that Annabelle's family and I hold dear, and hopefully fill your hearts with the same hope and joy that we can take comfort and solace in during this trying time.

Everyone you see around you in this room is a son or daughter of our Heavenly Father. He is the Father of our spirits. Our coming to earth is part of His plan of happiness for us, which allows us to receive a physical body in His image and continue to increase in wisdom and faith.

When Annabelle was born, and she was welcomed into this life by Bill and Evie, her earthly parents, she forgot her pre-earth life, and was forced to live by faith rather than by memory of God. To help her through life, God promised that His spirit would guide and strengthen her. Every time that Annabelle felt, and each of us feels the quiet comfort of His spirit, we know that God loves us and cares about us.

To this end, our life didn't begin at birth and won't end at death. Because God cares about us, we don't need to wander through life, wondering where we came from, who we are, and what we should be looking toward.

Our lives have direction because Heavenly Father created a plan that we can follow to return to live with Him. It is called the Plan of Salvation or the Plan of Happiness, and it is like a map charting our course home, no matter how turbulent the seas or how many detours and distractions we may encounter along the way.

God's plan for us is simple to understand, but it takes a lifetime to follow. Following the plan of happiness is easier when we do the simple things like reading the scriptures, going to church, praying, and serving others. Jesus Christ was the perfect example in following God's plan. It takes faith and works for us to be like Jesus, but it is worth it now and will be in eternity.

We come to this life to grow and learn and to be tested. That all sounds pretty taxing, but it's not hard to see how much joy we can find here on earth as well. Others will share with you their memories of Annabelle while she was growing up and sharing this mortal experience. While I will leave this to them, I do have to add that Annabelle was one of the sweetest people I have ever known. Having only three brothers, she was also the sister I never had. We shared a lot of good times together, and some not go good times too. But through it all, Annabelle was always the model of quiet, dignity and grace – unless it was a UVA football game in which case it could get pretty loud and exceptionally rowdy, but never mean spirited.

I know that as a parent of two children myself, that Annabelle was a source of pride and joy to her parents, her siblings, her grandparents, and all those that knew her.

One great part of Heavenly Father's plan is that all the happiness and satisfaction we get from learning and experiencing new things and all the love we develop within our families here on earth will go with us to the next life.

Just like our family bonds which can be eternal, we can also carry the knowledge we gain in this life with us after we die. Contrary to some representations of heaven, we will not be sitting on clouds, eating chocolates, strumming harps, and gazing at the face of God for eternity. Rather, we will have more opportunities to grow and challenge ourselves, as well as to revel in our family relationships, being re-united with all our ancestors who have gone on ahead of us. All these wonderful blessings depend on our faithfulness, here and now, as we work to keep God's commandments through our lives.

Our spirits are eternal. It is comforting to me to know that God has a plan for each and every one of us; that we lived with Him before we were born, and we will continue to live with Him into eternity if we choose. Our life on earth is fundamental to His plan, as is death. It is always sad when God calls our loved ones home, but we can be certain that their spirits live on.

When our bodies die, our spirits continue to live. The spirits of those who have received and lived God's plan will visit those who have not, teaching them and giving them the chance to follow God's plan.

Everyone's spirit will then be re-united with his or her perfected physical body, which will never die again. It is comforting to me to know that we will be judged and rewarded according to our works, and that those who follow God's plan will join him in heaven.

Many of us spend our lives looking for something to hold on to, something that will last. I was one of those who did that. I was raised to fear the finality of death, and to mourn those who had preceded me into it. That bothered me. It did not seem natural to do so. It also bothered me that there did not seem to be any real purpose to this life; surely there had to be more than seeing who could accumulate the most toys before we too had to die. I also wanted to know where I had come from, the real purpose of why I am here, and where I was going to go some day when I left this earth. I wanted this knowledge so badly that I spent years seeking it out, going from church to church, pondering and praying which was the true Church. I have also observed that some in this life look for answers on how to avoid growing old; while others merely seek fame and fortune. But we eventually realize that mortal life is temporary. We do grow wrinkles, our hair does turn gray, our six packs become love handles, friends and family grow old and die, the famous are soon forgotten, and wealth is lost as quickly as it is won.

As a result of the temporary state of life on earth, our hope and happiness lie in knowing who we are, where we came from, and where we can go. We are eternal beings, spirit children of an eternal God, here to have a mortal experience.

For this reason, our lives can be compared to a three-act play; pre-mortal life (before we came to earth), mortal life (our time here on earth), and post-mortal life (where we go after we die).God has had a plan for our lives since the beginning of the first act – a plan that, if followed, provides comfort and guidance now, as well as salvation and eternal happiness in our post-mortal life.

“For as in Adam all die, even so in Christ shall all be made alive.” 1 Corinthians 15:22.

As I said earlier, many of us are sitting here today with a great many questions in our hearts and minds. One thing that makes this life so hard sometimes is that we are out of God’s physical presence. Not only that, but we can't remember our pre-earth life which means we have to operate by faith rather than sight or memory. God didn't say it would be easy, but He promised His spirit would be there when we needed Him. Even though it feels like it sometimes, we are not alone in our journey. Quite often, it is a matter of moving too fast, not taking the time to listen to the small still voice inside of us that is providing us counsel, comfort, direction, solace, and hope.

We get sick, and sometimes loved ones die, often time leaving us to wonder why. We read about tragedies in the newspaper or hear about them on the news and sometimes may take a moment to reflect on the suffering of those impacted and then resume our own lives. We ourselves lose jobs, or homes, or suffer major disappointments, and then find ourselves asking why God allows us to suffer so much. It has taken me a great number of years to finally grasp that God takes no pleasure in our suffering or our difficulties, regardless of their cause, and that these trials can bring us ever closer to Him and even make us stronger if we but endure faithfully. It is comforting to know that God's own Son, Jesus Christ, suffered all things, doing so on our behalf. He understands our pain and can help us through our trials. When each of us has faith in God and His plan, we can be assured that there is a purpose to all that happens to us on earth. Our time here is short compared to our eternal life and is nothing more than a probationary period during which we too learn certain lessons, the necessity of which is sometimes only known to our loving Heavenly Father.

Coping with calamities can strengthen us and make us more compassionate. It can help us learn, grow, and want to serve others. Dealing with adversity is one of the chief ways we are tested and tutored in this life here on earth. Our loving Heavenly Father can compensate us for any injustices we may be called upon endure in this mortal life. If we endure faithfully, He will reward us in the life to come. Amazingly, with God's help we can experience joy even in times of trial, and face life's challenges with a spirit of peace.

Picture your hand inside a glove. The glove moves only when your hand does. Take your hand out and the glove sits lifeless on the table. This is an easy way to visualize what happens when each of us dies. Imagine that our body is the glove being operated by who we really are – our spirit. When we die, our body gets left behind, lifeless like a glove, but our spirit lives forever. Countless scriptures and personal accounts by prophets throughout time have told us this is true. Our physical death is not the end, but rather a step forward in Heavenly Father's plan and a time of indescribable joy for the person making the transition. Such is the case for Annabelle at this time. I know that she is no longer trapped inside that cancer ravaged and withered body, and that she is again young and beautiful, free of the chains of bondage that her body had become.

When we are the ones being left behind – the one losing a friend or loved one – a daughter, a sister, a cousin, a niece – the pain of that loss is very real.

This pain makes it difficult to comprehend that it is just as important to die as it is to be born, for the spirit to leave the body as for it to enter that same body. Mortality is a necessary prelude to immortality; it is by passing the test of this life that men obtain eternal life in the world to come. If there had been no creation, there could have been no fall. If there had been no fall, there could have been no birth into mortality. If there were no mortality, there would be no death. And without death, there would be no resurrection, and hence no immortality or eternal life.

It is my prayer for everyone here today that you will take comfort in the knowledge that you will see Annabelle again. And because of Christ's death, at some point her spirit and body, like all of ours, will be reunited at the time of resurrection, and made perfect never to be separated again.

I know that God lives, that Jesus is the Christ, and that the Plan of Salvation as I have spoken about it is real; that we are all spirit children of a loving and all-knowing Heavenly Father, who wants nothing less than for all of us to return home to Him, with honor, with joy, and experiences garnered from our sojourn here on the Earth, and I leave you these thoughts in the name of Jesus Christ, amen."

Success

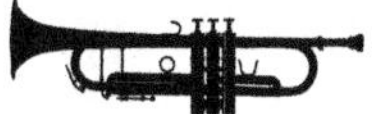

"The key to success is being able to discern between action and distraction. We all need to avoid the pitfalls associated with the day to day distractions that serve to rob of us of valuable time, energy, and attention to the tasks at hand. Put another way, avoid *futzing;* it is a tremendous waste of time."

"When you make it to the top remember that you did not get there without assistance. You did have help along the way. Make sure to remember to turn and reach down for the person behind you."

"The key to success is to act even in the face of intimidation."

"The price of success is always our own hard work."

"Don't go fishing for whales in a rowboat. Set and approach each task as an opportunity but attach reasonable expectations of success."

"The single greatest contributor to failure is doing nothing."

"Success is all about having a plan and executing on it!"

"Achieving success sometimes begins with taking a leap of faith even in the face of adversity."

"Success is the best revenge."

"You can practice and practice, and your weaknesses may rise to mediocre status. Better that you soar with your successes."

"Surprisingly, success in life rarely comes from making big, grandiose decisions. Rather, success is the aggregate sum total of small, seemingly insignificant choices that when compounded over time create the trajectory of our lives. Something we deem a sacrifice may turn out to be anything but a sacrifice but in reality, only a short-term down payment on a rich future blessing."

"Abraham Lincoln has long been one of my favorite presidents. A true pragmatist, he never shirked away from the responsibility of being the leader. Some of you may be a bit tired of not being able to get hold of people who have indicated that they want to talk to you, or having clients reschedule appointments, and feel like we are snake-bit for our efforts. Rather I will share with you a thought from old Abe: "Success is going from failure to failure without loss of enthusiasm." Much has been made about all the things that he failed at, or all the elections that he lost. What is often overlooked is the tenacity with which he lived his life. Remember, if you are interested in success, you must learn to view challenges as a healthy, inevitable part of the process of getting to the top. Keep the pedal to the metal, and let's keep the thunder rolling!"

"For most people, sleep is the time for their subconscious to process dreams of personal success and glory; for me it is a time for introspection and analysis. Such was the case this morning when I awoke much earlier than needed or desired with the thought of: 'To achieve complete success, effort and vision must be combined and subsequently nurtured in an environment of positive energy and attitude. Inhibitions and negativity must be shed and forgotten so that imagination and aspirations can be set free.'"

"Success starts with recognizing that the glass is half full."

"Success is a state of mind that begins with a dream, progresses to a possibility, develops into a plan, grows past execution, and ends at the finish line."

"Success is a reflection of your hunger and commitment."

Thoughts from a Life-long Cubs Fan

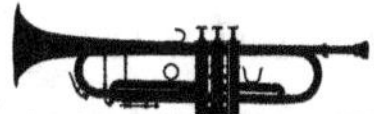

"Is there any greater example of faith, perseverance, and hope for the future than the heart of a life-long Chicago Cubs fan?"

"Faith is believing that there is always a seventh inning rally waiting to happen."

"Baseball is a wonderful thing because on any given day anything can happen."

"Two of the sweetest words ever put together: CUBS WIN!"

"A team's character is most evident when they are losing and enduring tough times – certainly not when they are winning, and everything is going right."

"On any given day, a mortal man can do the immortal and be memorialized for all time."

"If they are not hitting your fast ball, don't even think about throwing a curve or a slider."

"Isn't it amazing how you can go from being the goat one day to the hero the next. The key is to be on the field every day."

"Don't over think it."

"When you boot a ball, you have to shake it off and be ready for the next play."

"Greatness may be fleeting and contained within the confines of a single game that lives on forever."

"Even in the face of adversity and a 100 loss season, there are moments to be cherished."

"Always strive to be proactive. Don't go down on a called third strike. Go down swinging."

"Is there any greater childhood memory than Jack Brickhouse calling the game and making one victory seem like the turning point towards a brighter future?"

"Hey, hey, atta boy Ernie!"

"Way back. It might be, it could be, it is! A Home Run!"

"It's not over until it's over. Ever."

"A lot of people think that the blood that I have coursing through my veins is Artillery red...I would like to dispel that myth by proudly stating, without any reservation, that it is actually *Cubbie* blue that flows through my body. From the time that I listened with my dearly departed paternal grandmother to Jack Brickhouse call the games (long predating the more familiar Harry Caray) and witnessed the collapse of the '69 Cubs (8.5 game lead with 11 to play), thought the only thing that could exceed the joy of my daughter being born in July of 1984 would be the Cubs playing October baseball that year, to surviving with more than a little PTSD the *nightmare* of Game 6 of the 2003 NLCS until last night, I have been, and always will be, a Cubs fan. I thought being part of six Bulls championships, 3 Blackhawks Stanley Cups, a White Sox World Series win, and the Bears Super Bowl Shuffle were all special, but they paled in comparison to this week's epic Game 7 struggle in Cleveland. I was excited, I jumped up and down, and it was awesome!

But the World Series championship for the best team in baseball this year was much different, and far more visceral. I paced and walked and stood the entire five hours of the game. I even wore the same clothes both days for games 6 and 7! Three generations of Levins were in attendance, and what they witnessed was not always pretty. My Fitbit was working overtime to say the least. I jumped in the air, pumped my arms, and yelled my throat raw... when things were going right... and when they were going wrong. To come all the way back from a 3-1 deficit and to do it on the road was nothing short of magical.

In the 2016 presidential election that followed shortly after the conclusion of the World Series, I voted for **THEO EPSTEIN FOR POTUS!** If he can do it for the Red Sox [ending an 86 year drought] and now the Cubs [and their infamous 108 year drought], imagine what he could do for our country from the White House."

With the last recorded out, I jumped up and down only a couple of times, sent out another text – I was doing a running play by play color commentary for about eight members of my family scattered around the country – and then I finally sat down, became very aware of the perspiration that had soaked my shirt, and literally cried tears of joy, soaking the rest of the shirt. Fortunately, by that time the house had cleared out, and it was just my wife and our two dogs witnessing the waterworks.

When they carried retiring leader David Ross off the field on their shoulders, I saw a lot of tears on the television screen, and as for me, I could have been watching the movie *Rudy* which to this day still brings about the same result in my tear ducts.

What does the Cubs victory have to do with life? Probably nothing, except that it demonstrates the resilient spirit of Cubs fans who for 108 years began each year with optimism, hope, and a vision of glory. A Cub fan is loyal, faithful, and brimming with eternal optimism even in the face of adversity. Isn't that what we do each and every day as we attempt to educate people, burst their denial bubbles, and genuinely help them when they don't even realize that they need our help?"

"Win or lose… one must always be gracious."

"In spite of all the years of loss and frustration, one of my greatest memories of watching the Cubs play actually occurred at Dodger Stadium in April of 1976. Old number 7, Rick Monday, who played 19 seasons in the big leagues, made two All-Star squads, appeared in the World Series two times and was a member of the Dodgers' 1981 World Series championship team was the star that day, even though the Cubs lost the game by a score of 5-4. It was the bottom of the fifth inning when two protesters ran on to the outfield in left center field and attempted to burn an American flag. While struggling with their inability to successfully strike a match in the wind to in turn ignite the flag doused in lighter fluid, Rick Monday ran from centerfield, swooped in, and took the flag to the third base dugout.

The fans booed the protesters, gave Monday a standing ovation, and later in the season when the Dodgers visited Wrigley Field in Chicago, the Dodger team presented Monday with the very flag. He has kept that flag for over forty years, used it to raise over $500,000 for military charities, and will always be remembered for it.

At the time, I was a freshman in college and ROTC, coming to terms with my own sense of patriotism, and realized that Rick Monday, a former Marine Corps reservist, had put into action what we all should have been willing to do as loyal patriotic Americans. He displayed for me the moral and physical courage that I decided that I wanted to have from that day forward. Isn't it ironic that forty years later, we are dealing with athletes who will take a knee before a football game rather than stand to honor the flag that represents the thousands of servicemen and women who have died to protect their individual liberties?"

"There is a reason that baseball is America's favorite pastime. It is immortal, the rules pretty simple and straight forward, and allows grown men to remain little boys."

"Baseball for me will always be my grandmother, Ernie Banks wanting to 'play two,' and the excitement a win can bring even when mired in last place. I think it is the source of all the optimism that continues to serve me each and every day."

"I will never forget the very first time that I entered Wrigley Field. Walking up the ramp, seeing the green of the ivy on the outfield walls, the perfect green of the infield and outfield, and sight of the flags blowing in the breeze. It was a perfect day."

VISION

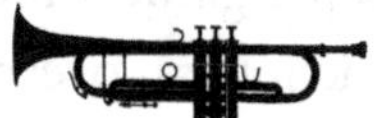

"The 1980 U.S. Men's Olympic Hockey Team won a game against a heavily favored opponent in the team representing the USSR. It was beyond a David and Goliath story and as a sports fan and patriotic American represented a true thrill of a lifetime for me, as well as the other American soldiers who viewed the game over Armed Forces Network in the Federal Republic of Germany. As captured in the Disney film *Miracle* this single game and the factors that led to it are studies in leadership, coaching, discipline, vision, and hard work. It remains an example to me of what true possibility thinking can achieve if we don't lose sight of the dream."

"The meek may inherit the earth, but this inheritance in itself will not make them great. Vision, determination, and diligence will be what allows these heirs to become great in their own right."

"Fast forward twelve years after the miracle on ice in Lake Placid, and it is now the 1992 Olympics in Barcelona, Spain. This was the site of the original Dream Team in basketball comprised of then reigning NBA stars. This team was an incredible amalgamation of talent. They not only won their games but crushed their opponents. In fact, the average margin of victory over their opponents was a mind-boggling 44 points per game. Since then, the term 'dream team' has been utilized to denote an overpowering line up of players or collection of people determined to accomplish a common goal. In fact, I have used the term many times in describing a team of leaders, whether professional or ecclesiastical in nature. Truly, it is a term that has been over used almost to extinction. I mention it now because it is important for all of us to construct our own personal dream teams of mentors, friends, teachers, parents, siblings, and those who simply care about us so that we can maximize our potential, achieve our vision, and in turn seek opportunities to be part of other dream teams and accomplish this same task for the significant others in our lives."

"If you are the leader, your vision has to be alive, and you have to embrace it to the point that when you hit the milestones along the journey to your ultimate objective, that both the route and these milestones are so identifiable that it is as if you have known them all along and that you have been there, if only in your mind."

"A great vision is based on powerful words that paint bold word pictures and elicit an emotional response. JFK's inaugural speech challenging us to all answer the call of service to our country and MLK's *I Have a Dream* speech are the quintessential examples of great visionary statements."

"A great vision will help you achieve more than you can possibly imagine."

"A great vision has to be alive. It must beat within the hearts of all the organization's members. It must be palpable and have a heartbeat of its own. Even the greatest *plan* will only speak to the head. A great vision speaks to the heart. It is all about achieving the emotional buy-in of the followers."

"A vision is more than a dream, it is a possibility that can become a reality when combined with perseverance."

"I cannot imagine even attempting to live any aspect of my life without a pristine vision."

"A vision provides our life with purpose."

"Values measures the rightness of direction; visions determine the destination."

"Without vision, the people perish."
In just about every one of my business plans, I have always referenced Proverbs 29:18.

"People criticize me for being *too* optimistic. But I don't know how you can create a positive outcome without first having a positive vision."

"I have found that most people are held back not by their actual abilities, but rather by a lack of vision that they want to create for their own future."

"A vision is the implementation of a dream. Without a vision there is no means by which dreams can become reality."

"Whether it is passing a tough exam, finishing as the top agency, or simply achieving a desired outcome, it all has to begin with a vision. The vision becomes the destination at which we seek to arrive. The long term plan, the short term goals, the one page business plan are merely the tools we utilize to achieve our desired vision."

"As leaders we have to own the vision. We have to create it, nurture it, share it, and lead the way to achieving it."

Winning

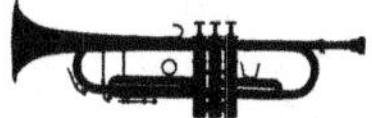

"Winning is merely a result of making the extra effort."

"More than just being about half full or half empty. A pessimist loses the game before he even steps onto the field."

"Quitting is never the solution to winning."

"If you are prepared, you will always have the edge. If you have the edge, and exploit it, you will win."

"Winners do the things that losers simply won't bring themselves to do."

"Being in the top three is great, certainly at the Olympics. But being Number One, the very best, can't be beat."

"Winning means so much more when it follows an arduous path or challenge that leads to the winner's circle."

"While winning is not everything, it certainly beats what is in second place."

"We may not have come over on the same ship, but we are all in the same boat now. It is all about working together as a team in order to achieve our common purpose."

"While winning is why we compete, it cannot come at the sacrifice of our integrity or the fundamental values of fairness and sportsmanship."

"Just as there are no atheists in a combat foxhole, it is probably wrong to pray to win; better that we pray to play and work and perform to the best of our ability and for this to be enough to carry us to victory."

Kids' Rebuttal

I was having dinner with some of my kids the other night and talking about this book. My son suggested that I should include the very quotes that *THEY* remember me saying the most which also adorn a picture frame that they created for a long past Father's Day. At first, I resisted the idea, but with a little prodding determined that if nothing else, it might be fun for them and maybe bring a smile to their faces when they read them years from now. So, with no further ado, here is the raw, unadulterated Don that they heard ad *nauseum:*

"What do you want, a medal or a chest to pin it on?"

"You and what army?"

"That's a good problem to have!"

"I would give my right arm to be ambidextrous."

"It'll put hair on your chest… on the inside."

"I have boots older than you."

"Back rubs in the front room can lead to front rubs in the back room."

"Bring a lunch and a friend if you are going to try to mess with me."

"I'm writing this slowly because I know you don't read very fast."

"I don't want to have a battle of wits with an unarmed man."

"It's hard to remember that your mission was to drain the swamp when you are up to your butt in alligators."

"We promise nothing, and we deliver what we promise."

"It's better to make dust than to eat it."

"Lead, follow, or get the heck out of the way."

"True North always has to be Integrity."

"Never has anyone done so little with so much..."

"T-H-I-N-K."

"Being overly optimistic never killed anyone."

"You can count the number of seeds in an apple,
but not the number of apples in a seed."

"Morgen, morgen, nur nicht heute, Sagen alle faulen leute."
(never put off until tomorrow what you can do today.)

"The meek shall inherit the earth, but not the mineral rights."

"At ease, keep your seats."

"At ease, I'll be in the area all day."

"What happened?"

"Who loves you baby?"
[Correct response: YOU do Sir!]

"Lotsa cheese, lotsa cheese!"

"Aaaah, a lovely shoyt."

"How lovely for all of us."

"What's for dinner?"
[my wife's favorite question!]

"Boom Time!"

"I don't remember eating any carn."

"eskoocha ya hacha"

"oooh wah- wah -wah!"

"Special lunch!"

"You see this thumb?"

"sto-MA-che–che"
(stomach ache)

"Guns don't kill people, people kill people."

"That's bad."

"Battle stations, battle stations, all stations this net."

"Bore clear on the battle star (base piece)."
[from my old Fire Direction Officer days]

"What's the name of that song?"
[when it is that obvious…]

"Tremendous drama."

"Easy does it Turbo!"

"Lighten up Francis."

"The key to Cavalry is flexibility."

"Skill is better than luck."
(motto of the Field Artillery)

"For the love of Pete."
[Grandma's favorite phrase. Who the heck was Pete?]

"Kaleem Kalemm"

"When you have dry toilet paper… you have a friend."

"Thank you, Grandma!"

"I've told you a million times not to exaggerate!"

"Ree, Ree, Ree, hit 'em in the knee,
Rass, Rass, Rass, hit 'em in the other knee."

"Here lies Lester Moore,
Four Slugs from a .44,
No Less,
Mo More."

Movie and Television Quotes the Family had to Endure...

For as long as the kids can remember, we have always talked in movie and television lines. Some of them we adopted and plum wore them out. Nonetheless they are part of the family lore, and hopefully will also bring a smile and a memory to those who read them. I suspect it will be our own version of Trivial Pursuit. It was definitely fun re-creating the list and having others contribute to this chapter.

"It's good to be the King."

"Have fun storming the castle!"

"There's no place any place quite like this place,
so this must be the place I reckon."

"On your feet soldier, I'm Colonel Potter."

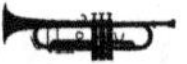

"You can't handle the Truth."

"You're killing me Smalls."

"May the Schwarz be with you."

"That will make you stupid."

"Mongo only pawn in game of life."

"Lieutenant Dan…"

"Ramming speed…"

"Was it over when the Germans bombed Pearl Harbor? No! When the going gets tough, the tough get going."

"You Mr. Blutarski have no grade point average…"
"Are you talking to me?"

"My name is Inigo Montoya and you killed my father. Prepare to die."

"Talk to the hand."

"Hey little fella, we know you're in there, and that you're all alone."

"Happy Hanukkah Marv."

"Splash the Zeros."

"To the Batmobile."

"Hold tight Robin, bat-turn."

"Atomic batteries to power, turbines to speed."

"There's no crying in baseball."

"You look mahvelous."

"Look what you did now you little jerk."

"Don't cry Shop girl."

"What you just said is one of the most insanely idiotic things I have ever heard. At no point in your rambling incoherent response were you even close to anything that could be considered a rational thought. Everyone in this room is now dumber for having listened to it. I award you no points, and may God have mercy on your soul."

"Sabatoogee."

"I'm a victim of circumstance."

"Merry Christmas Mr. Potter."

"Buffalo bagels."

"Helloooo"

"Bluecher!"

"Who's your daddy Gary?"

"McFly!"

"Cha cha cha."

"This don't look like Kansas to me Toto!"

"We don't need no stinking badges."

"Houston, we have a problem."

"Live Long and Prosper"

"You think DiNozzo?"

"No soup for you!"

"Remember…"

"Beam me up Scottie."

"You tell 'em ferret face."

"pulu cee ba goomba."

"Frank Burns eats worms."

"Kindness don't feed the bulldog."

"Gentlemen..."

"Happy new year to you... in jail."

"That's going to leave a mark!"

"What'd you do Richard?"

"You're not so tough without your car."

"My name is John Kimball and I love my car."

"You can do it!"

"Better to hold the phone than to get a kidney stone!"

"This is a very interesting situation!"

"Ladies and gentlemen, take my advice,
Pull down your pants and slide on the ice."

"Say Hey, that's lunch on me!"

"Happy Birthday Angel Birthday Boy."

"You must laugh all day. Yeah, my sides hurt."

"Forget about it!!"

"I'm on vacation!"

"The secret of Life – One Thing. You have to figure it out."

"Uh oh, my watch came off. It was a gift."

"Good job Cowboy."

"Woof!"

"Life can be a Do Over."

"And now for something you'll really like!"

"Nothing up my sleeve, presto!"

"Good afternoon Mrs. Cleaver...."

"Army Training Sir!"

"That's a fact, Jack!"

"Thanks for the gumballs!"

"Steve!"

"Whatever do you mean Gregory?"

"Fat guy in a little coat…"

"Until we meet again…"

"Book 'em Danno"

"Don't call me Shirley."

"Buffalo Gals won't you come out tonight?"

"Brothers don't shake hands, brothers gotta hug!"

"Does this look like a little weight?"

"You're gonna feel a little pressure…"

"The little engine that could. Chugga chugga chugga chugga, toot toot."

"Hot cocoa...I LIKE it!"

"I ---- on Jed Clampett."

"I know nothing."

"Colonel? Yo!"

"You're dead where you are standing."

Hello, I'm Mr. Ed."

"Build it, and He will come."

"Da plane, da plane. Hello Boss."

"What are you doing now Laura? Okay."

"Who's on First?"

"Wilson!"

"I can never beat those guys!"

"Spread out."

"Maybe it's a tumor. It's not a tumor!"

"Mr. Coach Klein, you got your manhood back!"

"Gatorade..."

"Without no tolls, we got no rolls."

"Bazinga!"

"Missed it by that much."

"Hello, Hello, Hello…Hello."

"Does the deer have any dough? Yeah, two bucks."

"George, do I pay you to be a canary?"

"There's going to be bursting?"

"That's quality H2O!"

"We go together likes peas and carrots…"

"You mean I have a brother?"

"I don't deserve ________"

"Merry Christmas you filthy animal."

"Sounds great Greg."

"I'm on the edge of my seat..."

AFTERWORD

Wow. Who knew that I had that much to say, or even had said that much?

In any event, in the course of assembling this compilation, more life-altering events that impacted our peace of mind, safety, and way we live life continued to happen around us. More History created if you will. If it went in the personal journal, it was worthy for consideration for this compilation.

What made this odyssey so special for me is that I discovered any number of writings that I thought were long since lost and was able to sit and remember the emotions that fueled some of them. Eulogies, fond farewells, acceptance speeches, congratulatory notes, as well as notes intended to simply inspire or encourage the heart.

In some instances, I was impressed at the profound nature of what I had said or written and *was left with the wish that I had followed my own advice and applied some of these principles more fully in my own life and relationships.*

I came to the realization that much like the lyrics of a song writer, these words are my opus and define who I am.

I am now driving a two-seater convertible, and some of the kids are convinced that instead of a semi-retirement present to myself, that it is really evidence of a *mid*-life crisis. If it is the case of the latter, then I must wonder what the writings of the *next* sixty years will address.

So how does one end a work such as this one? Death would be a finite ending, providing absolute irrefutable closure to the collection. But as was previously stated, this is supposed to be a mid-life review, so I guess it would be best to conclude with something memorable and Mel Brooks-like: 'God willing we'll all meet again in *Spaceballs II: The Search for More Money* – I mean, *Clarion Blast II: The Next Sixty Years On.*

Thanks for reading.

DJL

About the Author

Don Levin is the President and Chief Executive Officer of a national insurance brokerage and has been in the long term care insurance industry since 1999. Don is also a former practicing Attorney-at-Law, court-appointed Arbitrator, as well as a retired U.S. Army officer.

Don earned his Juris Doctor from The John Marshall Law School, his MPA, from the University of Oklahoma, and his BA from the University of Illinois-Chicago. He is also a graduate of the U.S. Army Command & General Staff College and the Defense Strategy Course, U.S. Army War College.

In his spare time, Don has published twelve other books in a wide range of genre, as well as countless articles and commentaries on leadership, long term care insurance, and personal development.

Don is very active with his church and within the community, and remains focused on his wife Susie, their five children, nineteen grandchildren and two dogs aptly named Barnes & Noble.

A native of Chicago, Don and most of the clan now reside in the Boise, Idaho and Northern Utah area.

Don may be reached at don@donlevin.com.

Printed in the United States
By Bookmasters